SHELF-ESTEEM

Sandra Kitain

Neal-Schuman Publishers, Inc.

New York   London

Published by Neal-Schuman Publishers, Inc.
100 William St., Suite 2004
New York, NY 10038

Printed and bound in the United States of America.

The paper used in this publication meets the minimum requirements of American National Standard for Information Sciences—Permanence of Paper for Printed Library Materials, ANSI Z39.48-1992.

Library of Congress Cataloging-in-Publication Data

Kitain, Sandra.
    Shelf-esteem / Sandra Kitain.
        p. cm.
    Includes bibliographical references and indexes.
    ISBN 978-1-55570-568-8 (alk. paper)
    1. Book talks—United States. 2. Self-esteem—Juvenile literature—Bibliography. 3. Social problems—Juvenile literature—Bibliography. 4. Elementary school libraries—Activity programs—United States. 5. Children's libraries—Activity programs—United States. 6. Children—Books and reading—United States. 7. Reading promotion. I. Title.
    Z1003.15.K58 2008
    028.5—dc22
                                                                                2008034737

To my grown-up children, Marshall and Lara, who inspire me;
to my husband Howard, who believes in me;
and to my mother,
who read to me and
ignited my lifelong love affair with books

Contents

Preface

The books and programming ideas in the pages that follow offer librarians, teachers, parents, and caregivers a unique way to help children develop their self-esteem. *Self-esteem* has been defined as "confidence in our ability to cope with the challenges of life" (Branden, 1994). *Shelf-Esteem* offers ways to help children develop that confidence and coping ability through reading.

In order for children to become good readers, they need both certainty of their ability to read and stories that speak to them in a personal way. I developed the first Shelf-Esteem programs as a grade school teacher and school librarian who wanted to help young people learn to read. To spark a genuine interest in reading, I had to find the right materials for each child. Once I matched the interests of the students with appropriate titles—and involved them in selection—even the most reluctant readers could find books that spoke to them.

I found that stories could also help my pupils deal with issues in their lives, from death to physical challenges to simply feeling left out because everyone else in the class was invited to a party. Children have a way of opening up when they identify with a particular character. Even the most sensitive subjects, when handled delicately by an author and illustrator, can provide an opportunity for adults to help foster self-esteem through reading.

Shelf-Esteem offers 50 programs designed to introduce children to books that relate to their personal lives and individual challenges. Each program is structured around a particular title and suggests additional titles on the topic: a "book hop" (see below), a classic, and a title for older children, for a total of over 150 self-esteem-boosting stories. These selections exemplify children's literature at its finest: well-written and sensitive, with subtle messages that allow the youngster to discover the meaning independently or with gentle guidance from an adult. They can be used as complete programs in the classroom or library or as reader's advisory tools. If a child has trouble with a bully, turn to Chapter 10 and consider a class reading and discussion of one of the books to introduce new ways to deal with the problem. Parents going through a divorce can be gently encouraged to use appropriate shelf-esteem books and activities with the child at home.

The shelf-esteem programs can be used effectively by librarians and teachers, as well as by parents and school psychologists. Partnerships between all the adults in a young person's life create a nurturing environment for the growth of confidence and academic skills. Teachers and psychologists can alert librarians to a child's particular needs so that the librarian can recommend suitable texts. The librarian has the opportunity to observe a pupil's independent interests and can communicate with the classroom teacher about using these interests to motivate the student.

Like other literacy tools, Shelf-Esteem techniques have the greatest effect when used early in a child's reading career. Research tells us that children's attitudes about learning solidify by age ten. Shelf-Esteem programs target preschoolers and students in the younger elementary grades, but their effects can reach through middle school, high school, and beyond. The skills the children learn become applicable to more difficult texts and more complex life situations as they move from grade to grade.

Shelf-Esteem's principles work in settings that go far beyond the model shown here. In my recent work with ESL students, I included information about their home countries from fictional stories, nonfiction works, and even cookbooks. Their interest clearly increased when I used these materials, and I could see their pride in their home countries grow.

Shelf-Esteem programs build a framework for success, book by book, by creating a series of successful, positive reading experiences in which the reader develops a connection to the characters. This connection is the emotional heart and joy of the reading experience.

A GUIDE FOR USING SHELF-ESTEEM

Part I, "Shelf-Esteem Handbook," offers programs on dozens of specific titles, arranged by topic. Each of the fifteen chapters covers a different area of emotional growth. Some chapters tackle subjects that all young readers encounter: self-confidence, friendship, bravery, courage, and emotions. Other chapters focus on more specific situations a student may confront: moving, new siblings, multiculturalism, physical challenges, bullies, and separation anxiety. The remaining chapters wrestle with tougher issues, including alcoholism, illness and death, fires and homelessness, and divorce.

Each chapter uses the same template to investigate and deconstruct the suggested books.

Full Bibliographic Information: The title, author, illustrator, publisher, year of publication, ISBN, number of pages, and recommended grade level.

Synopsis: A brief story description, explaining the plot and message.

Booktalk: A sample booktalk. Booktalks are as unique as the person presenting them, so these booktalks are just examples of one approach, not a prescription to follow.

Shelf-Esteem Connection and Idea Grid: The **Shelf-Esteem Connection** explores one core message from the book for a deeper understanding that will help children expand their confidence and self-esteem. The grid that follows the **Shelf-Esteem Connection** presents other possible areas of exploration:

THEME	MESSAGE	PLOT POINT CONNECTION	REINFORCING ACTIVITY	DISCUSSION QUESTIONS

This grid lists a few of the story's engaging themes and messages and ties them to a particular plot point. The reinforcing activity and suggested discussion questions help turn passive reading into active participation.

Book Hop: A book hop stretches a child's interest from one title to another. The book hop recommendation may be a fiction or nonfiction work on the same or a similar topic or may be another way of encouraging a reluctant reader to continue his or her reading experience. To make sure that the book hops are easy to find, only materials published after 1990 are included.

Classic Corner: This section highlights older or well-known works on a particular topic, especially those by famous authors or books that have won major awards. Some titles may be dated or out-of-print, but they are still worth tracking down.

For Older Children: With more sophisticated readers or students who read on a higher level, use these suggestions. This section's activities assume higher-level writing skills.

Support Material: A list of awards and honors the book has received as well as dates of reviews in peer-reviewed journals and highly regarded children's literature publications.

Part II, "Shelf-Esteem Essentials," expands on the possibilities presented in Part I. Chapter 16, "Exploring the Shelf-Esteem Concept," looks at the reasoning behind the Shelf-Esteem programs and book hopping. It examines ways to increase interest in reading and improve students' motivation, converting the "work" of reading into a positive experience.

Chapter 17, "Launching a Program," details the nuts and bolts of a good Shelf-Esteem program, including different types of booktalks, questions that encourage discussion, and creative activities. This chapter also includes an FAQ list on how to choose good books for fostering self-esteem.

Chapter 18, "Using Special Topics and Projects," offers practical tips on how to promote reading in a school setting or a public library children's room. It also includes ideas on engaging the senses and emotions with art, drama, and music.

Chapter 19, "Finding Shelf-Esteem Partners," presents ideas for collaborative endeavors including museum visits, interschool activities, parent-teacher conferences, parent-child book clubs, and book fairs. It encourages partnerships between schools and public libraries and developing connections with charitable organizations, teacher education programs, and principals and administrators.

Part III, "Shelf- Esteem Sources and Support," contains cross-referenced indexes, including subject, title/author, title/illustrator, and author/title. It also includes a complete bibliography and a list of additional selection resources.

Bruno Bettelheim's classic work *The Uses of Enchantment: The Meaning and Importance of Fairy Tales* says, "For a story to truly hold the child's attention, it must entertain him and arouse his curiosity. But to enrich his life, it must stimulate his imagination; help him to develop his intellect and to clarify his emotions; be attuned to his anxieties and aspirations; give full recognition to his difficulties, while at the same time suggesting solutions to the problems which perturb him" (1976: 5).

The books in *Shelf-Esteem* can enrich children's lives. I have seen firsthand the magical process that occurs when book, child, and librarian come together in the right way, causing a student to consider himself a reading success. Children who develop shelf-esteem use books as tools for information, entertainment, coping strategies, comfort, and the constant discovery of more wonderful books.

References

Branden, Nathaniel. 1994. *The Six Pillars of Self-Esteem*. New York: Bantam.

Bettelheim, Bruno. 1976. *The Uses of Enchantment: The Meaning and Importance of Fairy Tales*. New York: Knopf.

Acknowledgments

I would like to thank my editors: Miguel Figueroa, for believing in my project; Michael Kelley, for enabling me to turn my dream into a reality; and Eileen Fitzsimons, for her expert opinions and help when they were needed the most.

I am also indebted to Beth, Bob, and Steve, for enabling me to finish the work I started; my stalwart husband, Howard, for his unshakable belief in me and my project; and my passionate reading children, Marshall and Lara, who are now grown-up passionate adult readers, for helping me see my project through to completion.

List of Shelf-Esteem Titles, Authors, and Illustrators

PART I

Shelf-Esteem
Handbook

CHAPTER 1

Self-Confidence

1.1

Hurty Feelings by Helen Lester; illustrated by Lynn Munsinger.
Houghton Mifflin, 2004. ISBN: 0618410821. 32 pages.
Grades: PreK–2.

Synopsis
Fragility is a very sensitive hippopotamus. She is easily brought to tears and often turns a compliment into an insult in her mind. She meets Rudy, the rude elephant, and they face off on the soccer field. Fragility manages to give Rudy a taste of his own medicine. She soothes Rudy's battered ego and manages to calm him down because she is empathetic and knows how Rudy must feel after being insulted.

Booktalk
Would you ever expect a big 16-toed hippopotamus to have a sensitive side? Fragility, despite her size and appearance, is as sensitive and fragile as her name. Her feelings are so easily hurt that when a monkey tells her she looks nice, Fragility thinks she must look as nice and squishy as a soft, lumpy, mushy cupcake. When the giraffe tells her she has strong, sturdy legs, Fragility envisions her legs to look like the stumps of a piano. When an alligator tells her she has cute ears, Fragility cries because she imagined she must look like a human. And a hippopotamus doesn't want to look like a human any more than a human wants to look like a hippopotamus! What will Fragility do when she meets up with Rude Rudy, the Elephant who knows just how to get to Fragility's soft spots? How will she handles Rudy and turns events around to her advantage?

Shelf-Esteem Connection
Sensitive people can learn to develop a tougher skin. Rude people can sometimes learn new behavior by getting a taste of their own medicine. Mothers sometimes perform heroic deeds when caring for their children.

THEME	MESSAGE	PLOT POINT CONNECTION	REINFORCING ACTIVITY	DISCUSSION QUESTIONS
Physical Pain and Emotional Pain	Be conscious of when your feelings are hurt and when you have a real physical pain.	The animals in this book display opposite anthropomorphic traits than you would expect. (The animals are given human traits or characteristics.) Fragility's feelings are easily hurt. Fragility cries when she is insulted.	Make a list of all of the ways the animals in this book act like human beings.	What is the difference between a physical hurt and an emotional hurt?
Thinking Positively	Feel better by accepting compliments for what they are and thanking people for them, instead of hearing insults.	Fragility is told that her legs are strong and sturdy, but she takes it to mean that her legs are like stumps.	Divide a paper in half and write down the compliments that Fragility receives: she looks nice, she has strong legs, and she has cute ears. On the other side of the paper, draw a picture of how Fragility turned those compliments around into insults: Looking nice is transformed into being squishy as a cupcake, strong legs are turned into stumps, and cute ears are turned into looking like a person.	How can improving communication make certain that a word that was meant to be a compliment is not taken as an insult?
Soothing Others	Letting someone else know you understand how they feel helps soothe other people's feelings.	When Fragility sees Rudy is upset, she brings him wet washcloths and tissues.	Make paper-bag puppets that represent a hippo and an elephant. Cooperatively write a script that shows how the animals can communicate positively.	Can you think of some way you made someone feel better? When Fragility sees Rudy is all upset and crying, she brings him wet washcloths and tissues so he could blow his trunk. She tells him she knows just how he feels. How does that make Rudy feel better?
Soothing Ourselves	Protecting ourselves from getting hurt is a skill that can be learned and practiced.	Fragility thinks that being told she is nice means that she is as squishy as a cupcake.	Write down or dictate words that you can think of that mean squishy. Find other words to describe a cupcake by using the dictionary or a thesaurus.	How can we help protect ourselves from feeling hurt?

(Cont'd.)

THEME	MESSAGE	PLOT POINT CONNECTION	REINFORCING ACTIVITY	DISCUSSION QUESTIONS
Stereotypes	Stereotypes are challenged in this book when animals are not what they seem.	Fragility, the hippo, turns out to be sensitive and fragile. Rudy, the elephant, is rude.	Write or dictate the kinds of animals that appear in this book. Decide what attributes you world normally expect them to have. (For example, the monkey might be curious.) Then think of the opposite kinds of anthropomorphic traits these animals could exhibit. (For example, the monkey could be shy.) Then compare these traits to the traits shown in the book.	Can you think of a time when you thought something about how an animal would act or react and you turned out to be wrong?

Book Hop

The Complete Adventures of Curious George by Margret and H. A. Rey.
Houghton Mifflin, 2001 (60th Anniversary Edition). ISBN: 0618164413. 422 pages.
Grades: PreK–2

The adventures of the clever anthropomorphic little monkey who acts like a curious child; he leaves the jungle to live with the man in the yellow hat.

Monkeys and Apes by Gallimard Jeunesse and James Prunier; illustrated by James Prunier.
Scholastic, 1999. ISBN: 0590876104. 24 pages.
Grades: PreK–2.

A nonfiction introduction to the physical characteristics, routines, and indigenous surroundings of a variety of real apes and monkeys.

Classic Corner

The Hating Book by Charlotte Zolotow; illustrated by Ben Shecter.
Harper Trophy, 1989. ISBN: 0064431975. 32 pages.
Grades: PreK–2.

Miscommunication is often escalated when one person misunderstands a friend's intentions or misconstrues the words that are said. A child's feelings are hurt when she thinks her friend says that she looks like a freak. It turns out that her friend really said that she looks "neat."

For Older Children

Queen Sophie Hartley by Stephanie Greene.
Clarion, 2005. ISBN: 061849618. 136 pages.
Grades: 3–5.

Sophie has a list of what is she not good at, and her mother reminds her of what she can do well. Sophie is good at being kind. She finds out that it is not always easy to be kind to others, especially to the new girl at school or to the cross old woman, Dr. Holt.

Support Materials for *Hurty Feelings*

Awards and Honors
• Indiana Read-Aloud Book Award Nominee: 2004–05
• Bank Street College of Education, Best Children's Books of the Year: 2004.
• Pennsylvania Keystone to Reading Book Award Nominee, Grades K–6: 2004–05

Reviews
• *Booklist*: September 15, 2004
• *Bulletin of the Center for Children's Books*: November 2004
• *Horn Book*: Spring 2005
• *Kirkus*: July 1, 2004
• *School Library Journal*: October 1, 2004

1.2.

I Like Myself by Karen Beaumont; illustrated by David Catrow.
Harcourt, 2004. ISBN: 0152020136. Unpaginated.
Grades: PreK–2.

Synopsis

With good humor and without preaching, a young girl reveals her appreciation for her whole self, inside and out. The book is told in rhyming verse, so that the self-esteem message is delivered to children in a fun, healthy dose. The unnamed main character exuberantly expresses her positive self-image to the world, and by modeling that behavior, she spreads good feelings to all readers. She has the courage to say that she doesn't rely on other people's opinions of her to feel good about herself.

Booktalk

Is what someone sees on the outside really all there is to a person? What if you had spikes like a porcupine or horns protruding from your nose? What if you had beaver breath? How about purple polka-dotted lips or hippo hips? Would you be the same on the inside? Would you still like yourself? Find out how the main character of this book has the courage to say, "I don't care in any way what someone else may think or say. . . . I'm having too much fun, you see, for anything to bother me!"

Shelf-Esteem Connection

It is important to learn to love yourself.

THEME	MESSAGE	PLOT POINT CONNECTION	REINFORCING ACTIVITY	DISCUSSION QUESTIONS
Self-identity	Don't let others judge you. Form your own opinion of yourself.	The girl in this book does not let other people's comments or opinions bother her.	Using tracing paper, trace and then cut out the funny characters in the book. Put these	What are some ways you can keep feeling positive about yourself?

(Cont'd.)

THEME	MESSAGE	PLOT POINT CONNECTION	REINFORCING ACTIVITY	DISCUSSION QUESTIONS
Self-identity *(Cont'd.)*		She does not allow comments like "You are a silly nut" or "You are a crazy cuckoo bird" bother her.	characters on tongue depressors with glue and make puppets out of them.	
Liking Yourself	Learn to accept yourself, both inside and out. Accept your body and your talents.	The girl says: "Inside, outside, upside down, I like it all, all is me!"	Role-play using the insults in the book and then create comeback lines. In the book, the girl makes a snout of her nose. A good defense line would be, "My snout makes me smell everything faster."	Did anyone ever insult you for how you look or what you wear? What did you say? How did you feel?
Laughing *with* People, Not at Them	Being able to laugh with people, not at them, is a valuable quality.	The girl in this book takes what others say "with a grain of salt."	Create a funny caricature of yourself, exaggerating your features.	Can you remember a time when you used a joke or a funny face to make someone laugh?
Self-acceptance	Everyone has special distinguishing features. These features make us special.	The girl in the book says, "I like my eyes, my ears, and my nose. I like my fingers and my toes."	Decide what makes your eyes special. Describe them in detail. Then do the same for your nose, your hair, and your ears.	What are your favorite features? What are your least favorite features? How can you feel good about those as well?
Seeing Different Sides of People	There are different sides to each person.	The main character can be fast, and then she can be slow at other times.	Write down what you like to do quickly. Then write down what you like to do slowly.	Do you like to eat quickly? Is that because you want to rush off to do something else? Do you like to get ready for bedtime slowly? Why? Is it because you want to stay up longer?

Book Hop

Incredible Me! by Kathi Appelt; illustrated by G. Brian Karas.
HarperCollins, 2003. ISBN: 0060286229. 32 pages.
Grades: PreK–1.
A red-headed girl girl describes all the wonderful traits she exhibits and the qualities that make her unique, such as her "singular nose" and the way she whistles.

Classic Corner

The Biggest Nose by Kathy Caple; illustrated by Kathy Caple.
Houghton Mifflin, 1985. ISBN: 0395368944. 32 pages.
Grades: PreK–2.

Betty the Hippopotamus chides Eleanor Elephant about her long trunk. Eleanor tries various means to shorten her trunk. Eventually she learns to accept her features. She may have the longest trunk, but Betty will still be known as the one with the big mouth.

For Older Children

Activity: Take the illustrations in this book and write a script based on the storyline. Write effective comebacks for particular insults or unkind words.

Support Materials for *I Like Myself*

Awards and Honors
- Bank Street College of Education, Best Children's Books of the Year: 2004
- National Association of Parenting Publications Awards, Gold Preschool and Kindergarten: 2004
- Missouri Building Block Picture Book Award Nominee: 2005
- *Books and More for Growing Minds*: April 2004

Reviews
- *Horn Book*: Fall 2004
- *Publishers Weekly*: May 2004
- *School Library Journal*: July 1, 2004
- *Bulletin of the Center for Children's Books*: July 2004

1.3

I'm Gonna Like Me: Letting Off a Little Self-Esteem by Jamie Lee Curtis; illustrated by Laura Cornell.
Joanna Cotler Books, 2002. ISBN: 0060287616. Unpaginated.
Grades: PreK–3.

Synopsis

A young girl holds her head high and likes herself, accepting whatever the day brings— whether she is picked last for the team or even if she receives only a pair of socks as a birthday gift.

Booktalk

Can you still feel good about yourself when you've lost your front teeth, your clothes aren't the latest fashion, or when you make a mistake in math class? What about when you are the last one picked for the team? How do you feel when you do something brave or something nice for someone else or when you try something new? This book will show you why you should like yourself all the time and it shouldn't be dependent upon someone else or upon what happens to you.

Shelf-Esteem Connection

You don't need to depend on other people or events to decide your opinion of yourself.

THEME	MESSAGE	PLOT POINT CONNECTION	REINFORCING ACTIVITY	DISCUSSION QUESTIONS
Accepting People	Each person has special interests and one-of-a-kind qualities that make him or her unique.	The boys and girls in the book have interesting lunch boxes that reflect their special personalities.	Create your own special picture of a lunchbox that reflects what you like to eat. A display of these lunchboxes may be created in the library. Label it "Friends come in a bunch for lunch: Featuring Tuna Salad Islands, Mr. Cheese Curl, and your own creations."	What qualities make you unique?
Respecting Differences	Each one of us excels in a certain area, and these features should be highlighted.	Each person in the book has a medal, such as a "Medal for Bravery," "Medal of Best Friend," "Medal of Honesty," and "Medal of Polite."	Create a medal for yourself. Then create a medal for someone else to wear, praising a special quality they possess.	How do you feel when you fall and get hurt? Do you dust yourself off and start all over again? What if you aren't chosen first to be on someone's team?
Trying New Things	Trying something new is often a challenge, but everything is new until you try it once.	Grandma makes "octopus stew" and the heroine is pleased when she tries to eat something new.	Write about "something new" that you have tried for the first time. What new food have you recently tried for the first time?	Writing Prompts: How do you feel now when the school bus pulls away? How does that compare with how you felt when you were a kindergartener and the bus pulled away for the first time?
Understanding People by What They Read	What can you tell about a person's interests by the books he or she reads?	There are a lot of books with interesting titles in the main character's room.	Make up a bookshelf of titles for books in your room. Write about what these titles say about you and your interests.	Can you think of some titles of books in your home? If you could build an imaginary bookshelf, what would you put on it?

Book Hop

The Skin You Live In by Michael Tyler; illustrated by David Lee Csicsko.
Chicago Children's Museum, 2005. ISBN: 0975958003. 32 pages.
Grades: K–3.

This description of the unique qualities as well as the similarities of all children, regardless of race or ethnicity, is a celebration and cause for pride.

When You Are Happy by Eileen Spinelli; illustrated by Geraldo Valério.
Simon & Schuster, 2006. ISBN: 0689862512. 40 pages.
Grades: PreK–2.

A young girl experiences the love and nurturing that she needs from her family members so that she can grow confident and always be reminded of their feelings of unconditional love.

Classic Corner

Just Call Me Stupid by Tom Birdseye.
Holiday House, 1993. ISBN: 0823410455. 181 pages.
Grades: 4–6.

Patrick Lowe cannot read, and his self-esteem is damaged because of an absent alcoholic father and an unsympathetic remedial-reading teacher. His life is turned around when he meets his understanding fifth-grade teacher and his neighbor and classmate Celina, both of whom encourage and uplift him.

For Older Children

Liking yourself

You can be in charge of how you feel about yourself. The main character in the book says, "I'm gonna like me when I try a new task." Write about a new task that you have recently tried to do. How do you feel if you give an incorrect answer in class? What can you do to make yourself feel better when you do make a mistake?

Support Materials for *I'm Gonna Like Me: Letting Off a Little Self-Esteem*

Awards and Honors
- *Horn Book* Recommended Review, Spring 2003
- *School Library Journal* Curriculum Connections: A New Guide to Great Resources, Grades: K–3: October 2003
- *Books and More for Growing Minds*: August 2002
- *Baker & Taylor School Selection Guide: K–8 Fiction Titles to Order*: 2003–04

Reviews
- *Booklist*: October 1, 2002
- *BookPage Reviews*: December 2002
- *Horn Book*: Spring 2003
- *Kirkus*: July 1, 2002
- *Publishers Weekly*: September 30, 2002
- *School Library Journal*: October 1, 2002

1.4

Odd Velvet by Mary E. Whitcomb; illustrated by Tara Calahan King.
Chronicle, 1998. ISBN: 0811820041. Unpaginated.
Grades: PreK–3.

Synopsis

Velvet's name is unusual, and she always does things a little bit differently than the other children in her class. Nature fascinates her and she brings rocks, a sparrow's egg, and a milkweed pod for show-and-tell when the other girls bring dolls. Little by little, her classmates begin to recognize Velvet's talents and special abilities. She eventually becomes admired for her unique qualities instead of being ostracized for being different.

Booktalk (Narrative)

"Hello. My name is Velvet. My dad says the day I was born, the sun was just rising over the mountains. Outside, it looked as though the world had been covered with a blanket of smooth, soft, lavender velvet. And I like my name, even if you think it is odd. I like to collect rocks, and my favorite lunch is a carrot and a butter sandwich. When we have show-and-tell at school, all the other girls bring in dolls. I bring in something special from nature, like a milkweed pod. But when we had a drawing contest at school, even though I had only eight crayons to draw with, I won the prize for my picture of an apple. I may be different, but I am not odd. And I'll show you why."

Shelf-Esteem Connection

People are unique and deserve respect for their individuality.

THEME	MESSAGE	PLOT POINT CONNECTION	REINFORCING ACTIVITY	DISCUSSION QUESTIONS
Special Qualities	Our special qualities are what make us unique individuals.	Unlike the other girls, who like to show off their dolls, Velvet likes to show off her rock collection.	Describe your favorite collection by drawing a picture of what it contains or writing about it. Can you bring something from your collection to the library to share with others?	What do the things you choose to share from your collection tell about you?
Likes and Dislikes	Everything about us makes us special. Our likes, our dislikes, and our interests all add up to one special human being.	Velvet's favorite lunch consists of carrots and a butter sandwich.	Make a collage of your favorite lunch by cutting out the individual parts from construction paper. Put it on a paper plate and label the parts.	What likes and dislikes do you have that make you special?
Similarities with Others	Even though we have many unique qualities, we share many traits with others.	Violet draws using only eight crayons. But even though she is different in this way, she is like her classmates in that they all draw with crayons.	Create a drawing using only eight crayons. Write down the names of the colors you choose to use.	How are you similar to some of your friends and how are you different?

(Cont'd.)

THEME	MESSAGE	PLOT POINT CONNECTION	REINFORCING ACTIVITY	DISCUSSION QUESTIONS
Learning from Others	We can all learn from each other.	Velvet's classmates learned about a milkweed pod from her. She offered something unusual to the class that was uniquely hers and hers alone. In turn, Velvet learns to honor her unique qualities, as her classmates learn to respect her for her individuality.	Look up the phrase "milkweed pod" in an encyclopedia or in a science book, or have an adult look it up and read it to you. Find out what it is and what it looks like.	Can you think of something uniquely yours that you can offer or teach to others? This can be something that represents your special gifts, talents, or interests.

Book Hop

Ella, the Elegant Elephant by Carmela and Steven D'Amico.
A. A. Levine, 2004. ISBN: 0439627923. Unpaginated.
Grades: PreK–2.

Ella decides to wear her grandmother's "good luck hat" to her new school. She braves the teasing and the bullies at school and remains true to herself in the end.

Nikolai, the Only Bear by Barbara Joosse; illustrated by Renata Liwska.
Philomel, 2005. ISBN: 0399238840. Unpaginated.
Grades: PreK–2.

Nikolai is the only bear in a Russian orphanage, and he feels very alone until a woman from America comes to adopt him.

Classic Corner

Ramona Quimby, Age 8 (reillustrated edition) by Beverly Cleary; illustrated by Tracy Dockray.
HarperCollins, 2006. ISBN: 0688004776. 179 pages.
Grades: 2–5.

Individualist Ramona Quimby tackles the third grade on her own terms.

For Older Children

Respecting others' talents

Velvet is a talented artist who won a prize for her picture of an apple colored with eight crayons. We can display our individuality by sharing our special gifts with others and respecting other peoples' talents. Make up a program called "Showcase of Talent." Give individual students the opportunity to shine by singing, dancing, playing a musical instrument, drawing, doing a magic trick, juggling, or reading aloud. Discuss special talents that you can share with someone else. What talents do you admire in other people?

Support Materials for *Odd Velvet*

Awards and Honors
- Gillespie, John Thomas. 2002. *Best Books for Children, Preschool through Grade 6*, 7th edition. New York: Bowker-Greenwood.
- *Bulletin of the Center for Children's Books* Recommended Titles: January 1999

Reviews
- *Booklist*: November 1, 1998
- *Bulletin of the Center for Children's Books*: January 1999
- *Kirkus*: September 1, 1998
- *Publishers Weekly*: November 2, 1988
- *School Library Journal*: January 1, 1999

1.5

Shrinking Violet by Cari Best; illustrated by Giselle Potter.
Farrar, Straus & Giroux: 2001. ISBN: 0374368821. Unpaginated.
Grades: K–4.

Synopsis

Ultra-shy Violet does not like anyone to look at her at school. She doesn't sing in the school concert, march in the parade, or dance. But she is good at watching and observing others. When she gets the part of Lady Space in a play about the solar system, she saves her class play by helping Irwin (who was pretending to be the planet Mars) by using her sense of humor and her powers of observation.

Booktalk

Violet does not like anyone watching her. She doesn't want to march in the class parade. She doesn't make waves at the swimming pool. She doesn't sing in the school concert. She won't dance if someone asks her to. But one thing Violet is very good at is watching and making observations. She knows who can swim fast and who swims slowly. She knows what everyone brings for snacktime at school. She is aware if someone sings off-key in the school concert. Violet's classmate Irwin tells her she has hairy arms and that she should portray "deadly sewer gas" in the school play about the solar system. How do Violet's powers of observations help Irwin when he almost manages to sabotage and ruin the class play?

Shelf-Esteem Connection

Everyone is talented in a different way. Sometimes you have to look deeper to find the special qualities in another person, but that doesn't mean that those qualities don't exist.

THEME	MESSAGE	PLOT POINT CONNECTION	REINFORCING ACTIVITY	DISCUSSION QUESTIONS
Celebrate Individuality	Every person is unique and so are the countries they come from.	Violet is too shy to march in the "Carry-a-Flag" parade, but she is an individual who watches carefully and is able to make keen observations.	Plan a Carry-the-Flag Day at your library. Each child may be responsible for making a flag from the country of his or her heritage. Ask the children to find out more information about that particular country and its people.	How do you celebrate your individuality—your talents, your special gifts?

(Cont'd.)

THEME	MESSAGE	PLOT POINT CONNECTION	REINFORCING ACTIVITY	DISCUSSION QUESTIONS
Respecting Others	Let others have a chance, even if they like to do things differently.	Violet prefers to watch others than to be the center of attention. She is very observant.	Draw a picture of Violet when she is itching and scratching and twirling her hair when she meets up with Bully Irwin face-to-face. Place some words in a cartoon bubble to show what Violet wants to say back to him when he insults her.	Can you think of a time when you gave someone else a second chance? What did Violet want to say to back to Bully Irwin when he insulted her?
Being Observant	It pays to be observant. What you notice may help someone else.	Violet does not want to act in the school play because she is shy, but when curtain times come around, she helps save the play.	When you go out to the playground for recess, take a notepad and record some aspects of nature that you observe. Then report back to the class.	How did Violet feel when she "saved the school play" from disaster?
Accepting Yourself	When you are most comfortable, then others will be comfortable around you.	Mrs. Maxwell showed she understood Violet's feelings when she assigned her the part of Lady Space, who speaks from offstage.	Violet found out that she did not have to get back at Irwin by insulting him. She found another way to gain his respect, and she felt good about herself in the process. Write about how Violet was able to turn Irwin from a bully into a friend.	How does Mrs. Maxwell work with Violet's feelings by assigning her the part of Lady Space, who speaks from offstage? How did Violet feel when she saved the school play from disaster?

Book Hop

Speak Up, Blanche! by Emily Arnold McCully.
HarperCollins, 1991. ISBN: 0060242272. Unpaginated.
Grades: K–2.

Blanche, a shy lamb, convinces the theater troupe of bears that she is a talented artist and can make sets for their play.

A Play's the Thing by Aliki.
HarperCollins, 2005. ISBN: 0060743557. 32 pages.
Grades: K–3.

Miss Brilliant uses a student production of "Mary Had a Little Lamb" to solve problems with bullying and negative behavior in her classroom.

Classic Corner

Feelings by Aliki.
Scholastic, 1991. ISBN: 0590441981. Unpaginated.
Grades: K–3.

The comic-strip feel of this book lends itself to in-depth discussions about negative feelings that range from jealousy to sadness, to fear, anger, and then finally, to positive feelings of joy and love.

For Older Children

Mnemonics

Mnemonics are a good way to remember things: how to spell a word or a list of things. Violet's teacher, Mrs. Maxwell, helps the class remember the names of the planets by using the phrase: My Very Excellent Mother Just Served Us Nine Pizzas: Mercury, Venus, Earth, Mars, Jupiter, Saturn, Uranus, Neptune, and Pluto. Can you make up a mnemonic to describe positive things about yourself? You can even use the letters in your name as the mnemonic.

Support Materials for *Shrinking Violet*

Awards and Honors
- *School Library Journal* Best Books of the Year: 2001
- The Capitol Choices Committee, Capitol Choices: 2001

Reviews
- *Booklist*: August 1, 2001
- *Kirkus*: June 1, 2001
- *Publishers Weekly*: July 2, 2001
- *School Library Journal* Book Review Stars: August 1, 2001

CHAPTER 2

Friendship

2.1

Being Friends by Karen Beaumont; illustrated by Joy Allen.
Dial: 2002. ISBN: 0803725299. Unpaginated.
Grades: PreK–2.

Synopsis
Two very different girls find that the joy of being friends enables them to share their various likes and dislikes.

Booktalk
Can you become friends with someone who is so different from yourself? The girls in this book like different colors, they enjoy different games, and one is better at math, while the other girl is best at reading. They don't even like the same food! One hates mushrooms—one hates peas. But even though one girl likes mornings best and one likes nighttime better, they still like something an equal amount—each other!

Shelf-Esteem Connection
Even people who are not alike in many ways can still nurture a friendship. Being a friend also means retaining one's individuality.

THEME	MESSAGE	PLOT POINT CONNECTION	REINFORCING ACTIVITY	DISCUSSION QUESTIONS
Friendship	Even people who like different things can enjoy each other's company.	Even though one girl in the story prefers the color red, and the other girl likes the color blue, they both find that they like the color purple.	The girls find that they have some things in common, and that their differences as well as their similarities make for a better friendship. Take a poll in your library to vote on favorite colors.	How do their similarities and differences help form a better friendship? How do differences make a friendship richer?

(Cont'd.)

THEME	MESSAGE	PLOT POINT CONNECTION	REINFORCING ACTIVITY	DISCUSSION QUESTIONS
Retaining Your Individuality	Respect and revel in the differences and similarities you find among friends.	The girls find out that the key to what makes their friendship interesting is their differences. But their common ground provides for greater understanding.	Draw a picture of something that is unique about you.	What are the activities that each girl likes to do together? What do they like to do on their own?
Tolerance	Just because someone is not exactly like you does not mean that person cannot be your friend.	The girls learn that friends do not have to be exactly the same in their tastes, their interests, or their preferences.	The girls both like to read books to each other. Pair off with a buddy and read a book to a friend. Then have them read to you.	Does a friend have to be exactly like you? Can't a friend display different qualities?
Understanding	The girls come to understand that they can each explore different areas and still come back to common ground.	The author describes the girls' activities using rhyming words. For example, gowns/crowns, bed/head, nights/fights.	Think of some activities you like to do and try to describe them using rhyming words. (Example, bake/cake.) Then think of something you don't like to do. (Example, play ball/fall.)	What are the qualities to keep in mind when making friends? What are some ways of keeping a friend?

Book Hop

Lizard Walinsky by Roberta Baker; illustrated by Debbie Tilley.
Little, Brown, 2004. ISBN: 0316073318. Unpaginated.
Grades: PreK–2.

Elizabeth likes being called Lizard and Simon calls himself Spider. They build a special friendship that is put in jeopardy because Spider has to go to another school. Then Lizard meets Samantha, otherwise known as Salamander, and the twosome becomes a threesome.

Classic Corner

You're Not My Best Friend Anymore by Charlotte Pomerantz; illustrated by David Soman.
Dial, 1998. ISBN: 0803715595. Unpaginated.
Grades: PreK–2.

A disagreement strains the relationship of two best friends. They celebrate the same birth date, and they each end up buying sleeping bags as gifts for each other. They discover that compromise makes the best solution to their friendship's ups and downs.

For Older Children

Write about a special friendship you have developed over the years. How has this friendship survived the twists and turns of life? How are you and your friend different? How are you and your friend similar? Do you have similar interests? What do you have in common? What sets you apart?

Support Materials for *Being Friends*

Awards and Honors
- *Publishers Weekly* Children's Books: Spring 1996

Reviews
- *Booklist*: September 15, 2002
- *Children's Literature*: 2002
- *Horn Book*: Fall 2002
- *Kirkus*: April 1, 2002
- *School Library Journal*: July 1, 2002

2.2

Best Friends Together Again by Aliki.
Greenwillow, 1995. ISBN: 0688137539. Unpaginated.
Grades: PreK–3.

Synopsis

Author and illustrator Aliki wrote this book after having moved to London, England, from the United States. She missed her family and friends so much that she decided to write about two boys having a reunion after one of them had moved away. She describes all the emotions that the reunion would evoke—from joyful excitement to anxiety. Her feeling is, "Reunions make the world smaller and friendships closer." She dedicates her book to family, friends, and reunions.

Booktalk

Imagine that your best friend has moved away. How would you keep in touch with him or her? Robert writes letters to his friend Peter. What other ways could you communicate [e-mail, cell phone, instant messaging, text messaging]? Peter writes that he will be coming to visit Robert for two weeks. Robert misses Peter so much, and he is glad that Peter is coming to visit. But he also has some questions. Will Peter still be the same as he remembered him to be? Will he still like Robert's company? Will they still remain friends?

Shelf-Esteem Connection

It is possible to remain friends even if the friend moves away, but it requires special effort on both friends' parts.

THEME	MESSAGE	PLOT POINT CONNECTION	REINFORCING ACTIVITY	DISCUSSION QUESTIONS
Letter Writing	Even in the age of the computer, it is important to know how to write a letter.	Robert writes a letter to his friend Peter. Peter writes back that he will be coming to visit.	Librarian: Pair off students and ask them to write letters to each other. The partner could be someone in the same grade or a different	When was the last time you wrote a personal letter? Whom did you write it to?

(Cont'd.)

THEME	MESSAGE	PLOT POINT CONNECTION	REINFORCING ACTIVITY	DISCUSSION QUESTIONS
Letter Writing *(Cont'd.)*			grade. Then the library group as a whole could collaborate on writing a joint letter to a different grade level library group, such as YAs (young adults)	How do you usually communicate?
Maintaining Friendships	Sharing common interests is one way of solidifying friendships.	Peter and his friends make paper airplanes and then fly them in the park.	Introduce the Japanese art of origami to the students. Try some paper-folding. In keeping with the theme of being in touch, ask students to write messages inside their folded papers.	What are some qualities of a good friend?
Adjusting to Change	Value the qualities that you know and remember in a good friend, but also allow for changes.	When Peter comes to visit, he feels comforted that some things have remained the same. He finds the old toy chest and the puppets and the cars and blocks just where they always were. But he also notices some changes. He notes that Robert's bed is turned around, and that he has a new lamp.	Draw a picture of something in the book that has changed. Then draw a picture of something that has remained the same.	What other changes are noticeable in the book?
A Friend's New Friendships	There is always room for new friends without losing old friends.	Peter has a new friend, Alex. This makes Robert wonders about the status of their friendship now that Peter has a new friend. Peter wonders about Robert's new friend Will. Has he taken Peter's place as Robert's best friend? But all three get along and Robert says that Will is not his "oldest best friend."	Bring in photographs of your "oldest" best friends and write labels for them. Then do the same with photographs of "newest" friends.	Can you plan for a reunion of "old friends?" Invite young library-goers from your group last year to meet this year's new library group. Write invitations for a reunion.

Book Hop

My Best Friend Moved Away by Nancy Carlson.
Viking, 2001. ISBN: 0670894982. Unpaginated.
Grades: PreK–2.

A young girl is very upset when her best friend moves away. She wonders if she will ever have a best friend again.

Classic Corner

Lizzie's Invitation by Holly Keller.
Greenwillow, 1987. ISBN: 0688061249. 32 pages.
Grades: PreK–2.

In Aliki's book *Best Friends Together*, Peter and Robert wonder if their friendship will hold up over a distance. In *Lizzie's Invitation*, Lizzie does not receive an invitation to Kate's birthday party and is extremely disappointed. However, she finds that when one door closes, another opens. She meets a new friend, Amanda, on the day of the party.

For Older Children

Best Friends?
Write down how a friend of yours became one of your "oldest best friends." Is it someone who has been through many experiences with you? Is it someone you have known for a very long time? Do you share common interests? Draw a picture of one of your "oldest best friends." What are some ways you can keep up friendships when someone moves away?

Support Materials for *Best Friends Together Again*

Awards and Honors
• Cited in *Best Books: Children's Catalog*, 18th edition. 2001. New York: H.W. Wilson
• *Baker & Taylor School Selection Guide K–8 Titles to Order*: 1998–99
• *Best Books for Children*, 6th edition: 1998

Reviews
• *Booklist*: August 1, 1995
• *Children's Literature*: 1995
• *Horn Book*: Spring 1995
• *School Library Journal*: September 1, 1995

2.3

Bravo, Mildred & Ed! by Karen Wagner, illustrated by Janet Pedersen.
Walker, 2000. ISBN: 0802787355. Unpaginated.
Grades: PreK–2.

Synopsis

Mildred and Ed, mouse friends, find out that they have conflicting schedules that will keep them apart. They each learn to rely on their own resources. They find that they can manage successfully by themselves, but that the ingredients of a good friendship involve thinking of the other person, even if you can't be with them.

Booktalk

Mildred and Ed were best friends. They did everything together. But what happens when Mildred's violin recital is scheduled for the same time as Ed's art exhibit? How can the two friends manage to support each other, even though they cannot physically attend each other's performances?

Shelf-Esteem Connection

Support and understanding are really important to sustaining a friendship.

THEME	MESSAGE	PLOT POINT CONNECTION	REINFORCING ACTIVITY	DISCUSSION QUESTIONS
Support	Good friends support each other's separate interests and activities.	Mildred and Ed do many things together. They were making a kite together and getting ready to take it to the park.	Draw a picture of your own kite and then cut it out to get it ready for sailing in the wind.	How did Mildred and Ed think of each other when they were doing their individual activities?
Understanding	Good friends understand when there are times they can't be there for each other.	Ed has a special button collection that he spends time on.	Bring in an assortment of buttons to the library. Examine them and sort according to shape, color, size, etc. Count and graph the results.	What collections do you have that you can share with others?
Identity	It is important to maintain your own identity while still being close friends with someone else.	Mildred and Ed decide to do things on their own to get used to the idea of being separated on Saturday.	Make a list of activities you can do with others. Then make another list of things you enjoy doing alone.	Mildred thought how Ed would have liked making wishes on the stars in the planetarium. Ed imagined seeing Mildred's face in some paintings at the museum. How did they show that they were thinking of each other?
Enjoying Your Own Company	Sometimes people want to be with others, and then at other times, they would rather be by themselves.	Ed played solitaire, he went to the movies, he rode his bike, and he went boating. Mildred even went parachuting!	Mildred and Ed even ordered food separately. Mildred has spaghetti without the meatballs and Ed has peanut butter without the jelly. Think of other foods that you can separate (For example, bacon, lettuce, and tomato sandwiches; cereal without the milk; hot chocolate without marshmallows; french fries without ketchup.) Then draw a picture of these foods separately, and then draw another picture of the foods together again.	What do you enjoy doing alone? What is more fun to do with a friend?

(Cont'd.)

THEME	MESSAGE	PLOT POINT CONNECTION	REINFORCING ACTIVITY	DISCUSSION QUESTIONS
Inner Resource-fulness	Sometimes we can be our own best friend and help ourselves.	Mildred has trouble sleeping the night before the concert. She tries to read, she drinks warm milk, and she even counts buttons.	Write down some helpful ways you get yourself ready to go to sleep. (Example: reading, listening to music.)	What rituals do you have before going bed? Do you have a snack, brush your teeth, read a story, or listen to music?

Book Hop

Gigi and Lulu's Gigantic Fight by Pamela Duncan Edwards;
illustrated by Henry Cole.
Katherine Tegen, 2004. ISBN: 0060507527. Unpaginated.
Grades: PreK–2.
Mouse Lulu and Pig Gigi have a terrible fight through which they discover their individuality.

Classic Corner

The Recess Queen by Alexis O'Neill; illustrated by Laura Huliska-Beith.
Scholastic, 2002. ISBN: 0439206375. Unpaginated.
Grades: PreK–2.
The recess queen, Mean Jean, threatens the balance on the playground until Katie Sue arrives to threaten her domain. Friendship wins out in the end.

For Older Children

Nana Hannah's Piano by Barbara Bottner; illustrated by Diana Cain Bluthenthal.
G. P. Putnam's Sons, 1996. ISBN: 0399226567. Unpaginated.
Grades: 1–4.
Boys can pursue both baseball and piano-playing and still maintain their male identity. A young boy learns that his grandmother can inspire him to play the piano and he in turn can teach her about playing baseball. They each pursue their individual interests while learning about a new skill.

Support Materials for *Bravo, Mildred & Ed!*

Awards and Honors
• *Best Books for Children*, 7th edition: 2002

Reviews
• *Children's Literature*: 2000
• *Horn Book*: Spring 2001
• *School Library Journal*: September 1, 2000

2.4

Enemy Pie by Derek Munson; illustrated by Tara Calahan King.
Chronicle, 2000. ISBN: 081182778X. 40 pages.
Grades: PreK–3.

Synopsis

A new kid, Jeremy Ross, moves in down the street and quickly becomes an enemy. Dad gives the narrator the recipe for an "enemy pie," to be eaten only after he and Jeremy spend the day together. Spending the day together has the opposite result and turns Jeremy Ross from number-one enemy into number-one friend.

Booktalk

Today we are having a cooking class in the library. We are going to prepare a special recipe. It is called "Enemy Pie." What do you think are the ingredients of Enemy Pie? What would you want to put inside a pie to serve to your enemy? Would you put in earthworms or rocks? How about "ABC" gum (already been chewed gum)? What would you put in a pie to serve to your friends? Did you know that the only way to get Enemy Pie is to spend the day with your enemy? Not only that, but you have to be nice to him or her. What would you do if your enemy turned out to be a true best friend?

Shelf-Esteem Connection

Becoming a true friend is an art that needs to be cultivated. Turning an enemy into a friend is a skill that involves patience, tolerance, and an open mind.

THEME	MESSAGE	PLOT POINT CONNECTION	REINFORCING ACTIVITY	DISCUSSION QUESTIONS
Making Friends	There are ways to develop and to cultivate friendships that takes work.	The father says that his son's job is to spend the whole day with Jeremy Ross. His son recognizes that it takes two to build a friendship. The boys eventually decide that eating enemy pie turns out to be delicious! The boys have discovered that with patience, tolerance, and an open mind, friendships can be cultivated.	Draw a picture of something that Jeremy Ross and the narrator do together.	Why didn't the protagonist like Jeremy Ross at first? What did Jeremy do to get him upset? What does the boy's dad suggest he do about this situation? Why did Dad tell him that he had to spend the day with Jeremy, his enemy?
Empathy and Tolerance	Seeing things from the other person's point of view is helpful.	The main character envisions that Enemy Pie is made of earthworms and rocks.	Make a shopping list for the ingredients of your Enemy Pie, and look in the newspaper for ads for sales on these items. Draw a	Why didn't the boy want Jeremy to eat the Enemy Pie after all?

(Cont'd.)

THEME	MESSAGE	PLOT POINT CONNECTION	REINFORCING ACTIVITY	DISCUSSION QUESTIONS
Empathy and Tolerance *(Cont'd.)*			picture of what your Enemy Pie will look like. Describe how it would smell and how it would taste.	
Giving Others a Chance	Spending time with someone so that you can identify common interests is crucial in making and in keeping a friend.	Dad took out the recipe for Enemy Pie.	Each child may prepare a pretend recipe for Enemy Pie, listing their ingredients, providing cooking directions, explaining serving size, calories, and nutritional value. Make pretend pies out of Play-Doh or clay. Then the group could decide upon preparing a real Enemy Pie, which could be a pizza pie or an apple pie, for example.	What happened when the boys began to spend some time together? How did they help each other? How were they kind to each other? How did the main character lose his best enemy? What was his relationship with Jeremy at the end of the book?
Friendships	Friendships need work and attention on the part of both people.	The protagonist and Jeremy played on the trampoline and made water balloons and had lunch together. Friendships grow when two people are open-minded and give each other a chance. The boy's dad then ate half of the Enemy Pie. He displayed trust and positive thinking.	Make a list of activities you would choose if you were spending the day with your "enemy." Describe what you would have for lunch. When the boys begin to spend some time together, they actually become friends. Make up your own written recipe for "Friendship Pie."	What would be the ingredients in Friendship Pie?
Making Friends	Friendships don't always just "happen." If you want to make a friend, you need to be a friend, and these skills can be learned.	The boy didn't want Jeremy to eat the enemy pie after all. "I didn't want Jeremy to eat Enemy Pie. He was my friend. I couldn't let him eat it," said the boy. The main character has learned that he has made a friend by being a friend.	Draw a picture of the boy stopping Jeremy from eating Enemy Pie.	What are some ways to turn an "enemy" into a friend? Could you spend time with your "enemy" and learn more about him or her? Could you find out about your "enemy's" likes and dislikes?

Book Hop

Hot Day on Abbott Avenue by Karen English; illustrated by Javaka Steptoe.
Clarion, 2004. ISBN: 0395985277. 32 pages.
Grades: K–2.

Kishi and Renee do not want to have anything to do with each other, but the lure of jumping rope and eating ice cream changes their negative views.

Classic Corner

Stand Tall, Molly Lou Melon by Patty Lovell; illustrated by David Catrow.
G. P. Putnam's Sons, 2001. ISBN: 0399234160. Unpaginated.
Grades: PreK–2.

Molly Lou Melon is the shortest girl in her class, complete with buck teeth and a bullfrog-sounding voice. Her grandmother offers her sage advice about being proud of who she is and what she is, no matter what others may think or say.

For Older Children

Create a collaborative class book called "Friendship Pie." Decide what ingredients are needed and how it would look, taste, and smell. Everyone in the group can sign their names on the pretend pie. Send it to another group and wait for a response!

Support Materials for *Enemy Pie*

Awards and Honors
- A Reading Rainbow Book
- Children's Choice Book Award Winner, Second Place
- 2003 Peace Education Fund Children's Book Award Winner
- 2003 Children's Choice Book Award Nominee
- 2002 Children's Choice Picture Book Award Nominee

Reviews
- *Bulletin of the Center for Children's Books*: January 2001
- *Horn Book*: Spring 2001
- *Kirkus*: October 15, 2000
- *Publishers Weekly*, Children's Books: Fall 1997
- *School Library Journal*: December 1, 2000

2.5

Horace and Morris but Mostly Dolores by James Howe;
illustrated by Amy Walrod.
Atheneum, 1999. ISBN: 068931874X. Unpaginated.
Grades: PreK–3.

Synopsis

We are all familiar with the feeling of being left out of a circle of friends. At a certain tender age, everyone goes through strong gender identification to the exclusion of the opposite sex. This book shows that the best clubs to join are those that include everyone.

Booktalk

Horace, Morris, and Dolores are the best of friends. One day the boys decide to exclude Dolores and build a Mega-Mice Clubhouse for boy mice only. Dolores feels bad about being excluded, and she decides to build a girls-only clubhouse called the Cheese Puffs. Finally, they realize that working together can only be beneficial. So instead of having two club-houses, they join forces to create a joint clubhouse where they can all be friends. Can they all eventually learn to get along?

Shelf-Esteem Connection
Boys and girls can be friends with each other without having to intentionally exclude each another.

THEME	MESSAGE	PLOT POINT CONNECTION	REINFORCING ACTIVITY	DISCUSSION QUESTIONS
Including Others	Excluding one group of children and including others can cause hurt feelings.	The friends find out that it is more fun to play together than to separate into different groups.	Think of good names for the joint clubhouse, where everyone can join. A funny sign in the clubhouse reads: "Today's Topic for Discussion: How to Get a Fella Using Mozzarella." Write down some other funny rhymes. For example, "How to Find a Miss Using Only Swiss."	Can you think of a time when you were not included in something you wanted to do? How did you feel?
Treating Others Well	How you will be treated by others is a direct reflection of how you treat others.	The Frisky Whisker Club is more inclusive than the Cheese Puffs for the Mega-Mice because the Frisky Whiskers invites everyone to join.	There are pages in the book where bubbles are shown above the character's heads with words written inside the bubbles. This gives the book a bit of a comic book effect. Take the pages that don't have these words bubbles and write what the characters would be saying. Younger groups may dictate their thoughts for the word bubbles.	When did you treat someone the way you wanted to be treated?
Evaluating Clubs You Join	Boy Scouts and Girl Scouts are clubs that have rules about membership.	The Cheese Puffs and the Mega-Mice make their own separate plans.	Plan activities for the Cheese Puffs and the Mega-Mice to do together.	Think about the kinds of clubs you belong to and evaluate if they are "exclusionary" or not.
Teamwork	You can accomplish more with teamwork than alone.	When the Cheese Puffs and Mega-Mice boys and girls realize that they can make one clubhouse together, they work as a team and achieve greater success.	Divide the group into teams to develop plans for a new clubhouse with a new theme.	How can each group work together ultimately as one bigger group?

(Cont'd.)

THEME	MESSAGE	PLOT POINT CONNECTION	REINFORCING ACTIVITY	DISCUSSION QUESTIONS
Including Everyone	When people see a sign that says "Everyone Allowed" they feel included and part of the larger group.	Horace, Morris, and Dolores stay the best of friends.	Think of a name for the joint clubhouse that allows everyone to join. Make a listing of rules for the members of the clubhouse to follow.	How are someone's feelings hurt when there is a club that excludes them?

Book Hop

The Berenstain Bears: No Girls Allowed by Stan and Jan Berenstain.
Random House, 1986. ISBN: 0394873319. 32 pages.
Grades: PreK–2.

Brother Bear tries to exclude Sister Bear from a new club because Sister always wins at baseball.

Classic Corner

When Sophie Gets Angry—Really, Really Angry by Molly Bang.
Blue Sky Press, 1999. ISBN: 0590189794. Unpaginated.
Grades: PreK–2.

When children feel anger about being excluded, they express it in different ways. When Sophie gets angry she kicks and screams and roars and runs and then sometimes she cries. But when she stops and notices the world around her through her senses, such as looking at the rocks and the trees and the water and feeling the wind blow through her hair, she cools down.

For Older Children

The Secret Language of Girls by Frances O'Roark Dowell.
Atheneum, 2004. ISBN: 0689844212. 247 pages.
Grades: 4–6.

Kate and Marylin find their friendship tested as they have to deal with hurt feelings, peer pressure, and acceptance issues.

Support Materials for *Horace and Morris but Mostly Dolores*

Awards and Honors
• Bank Street College of Education, Best Children's Books of the Year: 2000
• Books About Relationships and Community Building, Children's Book Council: 2002
• Editor's Choice, Books for Youth, American Library Association: 1999
• Bank Street College of Education, Books to Read Aloud to Children of All Ages: 2003
• *Children's Catalog*, 18th edition: 2001. New York: H.W. Wilson
• School Library Journal Best Books: 1999

Reviews
• *Booklist*, Book Review Stars: February 15, 1999
• *Horn Book*: Fall, 1999

- *Kirkus*, Book Review Stars: 1999
- *School Library Journal*, Book Review Stars: March, 1999
- *Bulletin of the Center for Children's Books*: March, 1999

2.6

How to Lose All Your Friends by Nancy Carlson.
Viking, 1994. ISBN: 0670849065. Unpaginated.
Grades: PreK–2.

Synopsis

By not sharing, by being cranky, by being selfish, by being a bully, by being mean, by being a poor sport, by being a tattletale, and by whining, a girl discovers that she will lose her friends. This guidebook offers indirect instruction on actually *how* to behave to be a good friend.

Booktalk

How many friends would you have if are always gloomy and never smile; if you refuse to share and pick on kids smaller than you; if you are a poor sport, tattletale, and always whine? Discover how to make friends, become a good friend, and keep a good friend.

Shelf-Esteem Connection

Learning how to lose all of your friends teaches ways to keep your friendships strong. Learning how *not* to behave can be as important as learning the proper way to act.

THEME	MESSAGE	PLOT POINT CONNECTION	REINFORCING ACTIVITY	DISCUSSION QUESTIONS
Being Unselfish	By being unselfish, you willingly share with others.	The girl in this book does not display unselfish traits by keeping things for herself.	Make a list of ways of how someone can be sharing vs. how someone can be selfish at school, the library, or at home.	Think of a way that you were unselfish and how you felt about sharing.
Being Kind	Being kind involves making compromises, being patient, taking turns, and sharing.	Turn the negative ways the girl in this book reacts into positive reactions to show how attitudes can change through effort.	Write down ways to turn a negative feeling or reaction into a positive one. Role play various parts of the book and offer positive solutions to negativity. Write down each negative feeling, thought, or emotion expressed in the book on an index card. Then turn the card over and write a corresponding positive emotion, thought, or feeling.	Ask the group how negatively phrased statements could be scripted in a positive way.

(Cont'd.)

THEME	MESSAGE	PLOT POINT CONNECTION	REINFORCING ACTIVITY	DISCUSSION QUESTIONS
Changing Perspective	It helps to try to see how you behave from the other person's point of view.	To prove her point of how to be a friend, this author wrote down ways of how NOT to be a good friend.	Write an instruction book of how "not" to do something well, in the style of this book. (Example: How to Be a Poor Sport.)	How can you be helped to see things from someone else's point of view?
Sharing Your Feelings	Make sure the other person knows how you feel. Not only can you show them how you feel, but you must use your words to tell them.	The main character in this book is not making friends. To have a friend, you must *be* a friend.	Divide a paper in half and draw or write "friendly" behaviors and on the other half, draw or write "not friendly" behaviors.	Can you think of a time when you shared your feelings about something special?
Using Words to Express Feelings	Words are more powerful than fists. Words are the best way to communicate.	The negative attitudes the protagonist displays are: not sharing, being cranky, being selfish, being a bully, being mean, being a poor sport, being a tattletale, and whining.	Create a word wall with words that express displeasure vs. words that show agreement. For example, whining and complaining words would be on the displeasure word wall, and cooperation and sharing words would be on the agreement word wall.	Do you feel better when you tell someone exactly how you feel?

Book Hop

Humble Pie by Jennifer Donnelly; illustrated by Stephen Gammell.
Atheneum, 2002. ISBN: 0689844352. Unpaginated.
Grades: PreK–2.

Theo is selfish, rotten, and lazy so his grandmother puts him inside a pie to teach him a lesson.

Classic Corner

King of the Playground by Phyllis Reynolds Naylor; illustrated by Nola Langner Malone.
Alladin, 1994. ISBN: 0689718020. 32 pages.
Grades: PreK–2.

Kevin learns how to cope with Sammy, who boasts that he is the King of the Playground. By working together, they find common ground and a way to cooperate with one another.

For Older Children

Make up your own list of how to lose all of your friends. Then make a list of how to keep all of your friends.

Support Materials for *How to Lose All Your Friends*

Awards and Honors
• *Best Books for Children*, 6th edition: 1998

Reviews
- *Booklist*: September 1, 1994
- *Children's Literature*: 1997
- *Kirkus*: August 15, 1994
- *Parent Council*: Volume 5, 1997
- *School Library Journal*: October 1994

2.7

Wanted: Best Friend by A. M. Monson; illustrated by Lynn Munsinger.
Dial, 1997. ISBN: 0803714858. Unpaginated.
Grades: PreK–2.

Synopsis
After a disagreement with Mouse, Cat decides to advertise in the newspaper for a new best friend. Mole, Otter, and Raccoon all try out, with unexpected results. After much give and take, to Cat's surprise, Mouse turns out to be his favorite best friend after all.

Booktalk
Would you ever put an ad in the newspaper for a best friend? That is just what Cat did when he and Mouse had a disagreement over whether to play checkers for the fourth time or change to playing Crazy Eights. Mole answers Cat's ad, but he is pretty hungry. He proceeds to raid the refrigerator for soda, peanut butter, bananas, crackers, an ice cream bar, and pretzels. What do you suppose happens to all of that food? Next, Otter applies for the job as "new best friend." Otter likes to play ball, and he arrives with a baseball, a basketball, a softball, a football, and a soccer ball. What does Otter do to Cat's house with all of that sports equipment? Raccoon rings Cat's doorbell next and applies for the best friend job. But he rides a skateboard and laughs at Cat when Cat tries to skateboard. Who do you think Cat calls back to his house again to be his best friend?

Shelf-Esteem Connection
Your own best pal could be right under your nose, and you don't even know it!

THEME	MESSAGE	PLOT POINT CONNECTION	REINFORCING ACTIVITY	DISCUSSION QUESTIONS
Qualities Valued in a Friend	Everyone has different traits that they value in a friend.	Cat wants a friend who likes to play games.	Write or dictate a personal ad for the newspaper advertising for a best friend. Explain the games you want to play and the qualities you are looking for in a friend.	Who knows how to play Crazy Eights and checkers? Who can write down the steps to teach others those games?
Compromise	Sometimes we have to give in a little to keep a friendship going.	Cat said to Mouse, "Please come back. Willing to play Crazy Eights,	Draw a picture of what made otter, raccoon, and mole unsuitable friends for Cat.	How important is compromise in having and keeping a friend?

(Cont'd.)

THEME	MESSAGE	PLOT POINT CONNECTION	REINFORCING ACTIVITY	DISCUSSION QUESTIONS
Compromise (Cont'd.)		Cat." In the beginning of the book, cat didn't want to play Crazy Eights anymore. But at the end of the book, he says, "You're my best friend."		
Maintaining Friendships	We need to show our friends that they can count on us.	Cat was happy that mouse was so tidy, that he never threw things around the house, and that he didn't skateboard.	Write or dictate a thank you note to mouse extolling all of his good qualities.	What are some ways to keep a friend?
Sharing Interests	Similar interests help to keep friends together.	Cat and mouse enjoy the same games, and that helps them keep up their friendship.	Divide a paper in half. Write down or draw the things that cat and mouse like to do together. Then on the other side of the paper, write or draw what raccoon, otter, and mole like to do that cat does not enjoy.	Why do cat and mouse get along so well? They like to play the same games, for one.
Giving Others a Chance	It is good to interact with other people and give them a chance to get to know you.	Cat still played with mole, otter, and raccoon even though his favorite friend was mouse.	Draw a picture of a game you would like to play with someone OTHER than your best friend.	What made Otter, Raccoon, and Mole unsuitable as best friends for Cat?

Book Hop

How to be a Good Dog by Gail Page.
Bloomsbury, 2006. ISBN: 1582346836. Unpaginated.
Grades: PreK–2.

Cat tries to get Dog to act in a way that would lead Mrs. Birdhead to approve of him.

Classic Corner

A Splendid Friend, Indeed by Suzanne Bloom.
Boyds Mills, 2005. ISBN: 1590782860. Unpaginated.
Grades: PreK–2.

An instant classic about the friendship between a polar bear and a goose.

For Older Children

The Storm by Cynthia Rylant; illustrated by Preston McDaniels.
Alladin, 2003. ISBN: 068984882X. 80 pages.
Grades: 1–4.

Pandora the cat lives in a lighthouse by herself. One day, during a storm, she rescues Seabold the dog, and they begin a life together with three mice.

Support Materials for *Wanted: Best Friend*

Awards and Honors
• *Baker & Taylor School Selection Guide K–8 Titles to Order*: 1998–99

Reviews
• *Booklist*: December 15, 1996
• *Children's Literature*: 1997
• *Horn Book*: Fall 1997
• *Kirkus*: December 15, 1997
• *Publishers Weekly*: December 1996

CHAPTER 3

Bravery

3.1

Amber Was Brave, Essie Was Smart by Vera B. Williams.
Greenwillow, 2001. ISBN: 0060294604. 72 pages.
Grades: 2–3.

Synopsis
Sisters Amber and Essie find their lives turned upside down when their father is incarcerated, which forces their mother to work full-time and teaches the girls lessons in self-reliance. Essie becomes smarter when she reads library books and learns how to thread a needle and cook cheese sandwiches. Amber learns bravery by asking the grocery man to let the girls pay for food on credit, not panicking when she sees a rat under the sink, and singing a song Daddy wrote, even though it might be a painful and sad song. Amber and Essie learn how to share their new skills to comfort one another.

Booktalk
The title of this book is *Amber Was Brave, Essie Was Smart*. How was Amber brave? Well, for one thing, she wasn't too timid to get the grocery man to trust her when she didn't have enough money to pay for milk. She wasn't even afraid of the rat in the wall under the sink in their kitchen! How was Essie smart? Essie could read library books, and she could thread a needle. Essie understood what happened when a policeman came to take their daddy to jail. Essie and Amber are sisters who face a lot of bad times, but they also share good times together. What does the cover of the book show you about how Amber and Essie feel about each other?

Shelf-Esteem Connection
Parents always love their children—even if they have to live away from the rest of the family.

THEME	MESSAGE	PLOT POINT CONNECTION	REINFORCING ACTIVITY	DISCUSSION QUESTIONS
Maintaining Balance	It is possible to have fun even when times are difficult.	Amber makes up a simple poem about daddy, using one word per line. It is called the "Daddy Song."	Make up a poem as Amber did when she missed her father. Use one word per line, saying the person's name, and then write a descriptive word about the person.	Can you make up lists of words that describe members of your family?
Dependence and Independence	Certain issues have to be faced alone; other times there are people to rely on for support and comfort.	The girls had to make independent decisions. For example, what could they eat?	Make up a pretend shopping list of what you would like to buy if you had to buy your own breakfast.	What would you plan to eat for breakfast? What foods would you need to buy?
Team Effort	Working together and pooling resources to try to offer family members strength and compassion allows one's positive traits to shine through.	Essie and Amber stay warm and comfort each other by making a "Best Sandwich." They have a fat pillow and Wilson the Bear in their Sandwich.	Draw a picture of your "Best Sandwich." Tell what ingredients you would put in your sandwich.	How have you worked together cooperatively with someone else in your family?
Resilience	Everyone can learn ways to stay strong through bad times.	Wilson the Bear is comforting to Essie and Amber when they are upset or scared. The characters help each other through their resilient spirit.	Draw a picture of a special teddy bear or stuffed animal that makes you feel better when you are upset or scared.	What comforts you when you are upset or scared?
Keeping Memories Alive	When people are far away, even if they have done something bad, their families want to remember them, and their families want to be remembered by them.	Amber cuts off her braids to send to Daddy in jail so he will remember her.	Describe in words or in a picture what you would send to a loved one who is far away.	What is it about you that you would like someone to remember?

Book Hop

A Chair for My Mother by Vera B. Williams.
Greenwillow, 1982. ISBN: 068800914X. 32 pages.
Grades: PreK–3.

The characters have to deal with the aftermath of a fire in their apartment. Williams, also author of *Amber Was Brave, Essie Was Smart*, explores how resilient children handle difficult life circumstances.

Classic Corner

Sheila Rae, the Brave by Kevin Henkes.
Greenwillow, 1987. ISBN: 0688071554. 32 pages.
Grades: PreK–2.

Sheila Rae is a very confident mouse who isn't afraid of the dark, thunder, lightning, or even a monster in her closet. But one day, she gets lost on her way home, and her sister Louise, the sibling Sheila calls "Scaredy-cat," helps Sheila find her way back home.

For Older Children

Dear Author: Letters of Hope edited by Joan F. Kaywell.
Philomel, 2007. ISBN: 0399237054. 222 pages.
Grades: 6 and up.

Teens write letters to their favorite authors asking for advice on life's tough decisions and choices.

Activity: Start a gratitude journal by making a list of the things for which you are thankful.

Support Materials for *Amber Was Brave, Essie Was Smart*

Awards and Honors
• Bank Street College of Education, Best Children's Books of the Year: 2002
• American Library Association Notable Books for Children: 2002
• NAIBA Book of the Year Award Winner: 2002
• *New York Times* Notable Books: 2001
• *School Library Journal* Best Books: 2001

Reviews
• *Horn Book*: Spring 2002
• *Booklist*, Book Review Stars: September 15, 2001
• *Bulletin of the Center for Children's Books*: September 2001
• *Publishers Weekly*, Book Review Stars: August 27, 2001
• *School Library Journal*, Book Review Stars: September 1, 2001

3.2

The Bravest of Us All by Marsha Diane Arnold; illustrated by Brad Sneed.
Dial, 2000. ISBN: 0803724098. Unpaginated.
Grades: K–3.

Synopsis
Ruby Jane thinks that her sister Velma Jean is the bravest person she knows. Ruby Jane is afraid of almost everything. Velma Jean is not afraid of anything—until a storm comes. Velma Jean is so afraid of going into the storm cellar that she would rather take a chance with the tornado. Then Ruby Jane gets to show her sister the true meaning of bravery.

Booktalk

Courage can be found in many forms. Velma Jean was not afraid of anything. Her sister Ruby Jane says she is afraid of almost anything. Ruby Jane used to go down in the storm cellar to play and get cool, but Velma Jean never went in there because she was too busy. One day a storm came up that started to look like a tornado. Then everyone had to hide in the storm cellar. Everyone did, except for Velma Jean. She said, "That storm cellar will swallow me into the ground. I'll take my chances with the tornado." Ruby Jane promises her sister that the storm cellar will not swallow her up and tells her that she will not go down into it without her. Read the book to find out if Velma Jean follows her sister to safety.

Shelf-Esteem Connection

There are many ways to show bravery. Different people are afraid of different things, but they can also be courageous in different circumstances.

THEME	MESSAGE	PLOT POINT CONNECTION	REINFORCING ACTIVITY	DISCUSSION QUESTIONS
New Experiences	It is best not to be afraid of new experiences. Sometimes calling something by a different name might make it less scary.	Mama calls the storm cellar the root cellar because she stores root vegetables there. There are jars of beets, potatoes, and carrots.	*Librarian:* Encourage the children to try something new. Invite them into your pretend root cellar (shut the lights in the library room) and sample root vegetables. Root vegetables can include carrots, beets, and turnips.	Do you remember a time when you tried something new?
Recycling	There are many ways to create something new from something old—recycle, for example.	Velma Jean and Ruby Jane played with Mama's buttons cut from worn clothing.	Make a picture frame using a cardboard frame, old buttons, and glue.	How did you recycle something old into something useable?
Bravery	There are many types of bravery.	Ruby Jane liked to cool off in the storm cellar. Velma Jean fears going down to the storm cellar. In the storm cellar, Ruby Jane chooses the family's dinner vegetable.	Describe in words or a drawing how the cellar would look to you. Choose and describe the family's dinner vegetable.	How have you shown your bravery with your family?
Heroes	There is a difference between being a hero and being daring.	Velma Jean says she is brave because she crosses a sandbar patch, she can swim in the horse tank, and she can even ride a new colt. But Ruby Jane finds out she is a real hero when she saves her sister's life by convincing her to go into the storm cellar.	*Librarian:* Help the children dictate a chart that shows instances in which someone displays daring behavior instead of heroic behavior. A whiteboard is useful for this exercise.	What is the difference between someone who is daring and someone who is a true hero?

(Cont'd.)

THEME	MESSAGE	PLOT POINT CONNECTION	REINFORCING ACTIVITY	DISCUSSION QUESTIONS
New Experiences	It is a good idea to expect the unexpected and accept it when it comes.	When people told Velma Jean she was brave, she said, "Let me tell you about the day my little sister looked a tornado in the face."	Describe, in writing, someone whom you admire. Then write or tell about how *you* could actually be that person's unexpected hero.	Can you think of a time when you did something that was not expected and you helped someone else?

Book Hop

The Enormous Turnip by Alexei Tolstoy; illustrated by Scott Goto.
Harcourt, 2002. ISBN: 0152045848. Unpaginated.
Grades: K–2.

This cumulative fable tells the story of an old man who plants a turnip that is so enormous that everyone needs to help him pull it out of the ground.

Joseph Had a Little Overcoat by Simms Taback.
Viking, 1999. ISBN: 0670878553. Unpaginated.
Grades: PreK–3.

This story is based on a Yiddish folk song about a tailor who is able to recycle a very old overcoat many times, each time turning it into something smaller—until finally it becomes a song.

Classic Corner

Brave Irene by William Steig.
Farrar, Straus & Giroux, 1986. ISBN: 0374309477. 32 pages.
Grades: K–2.

Irene's mother, Mrs. Bobbin, sews a gown for the Duchess. It must be delivered to the palace right away. Irene's mother doesn't feel well, so Irene volunteers to make the delivery herself. She goes out in a blizzard, and the strong wind carries the gown away from her. Ultimately, she finds the gown stuck to a tree trunk, and she makes her triumphant delivery.

For Older Children

Bravery Soup by Maryann Cocca-Leffler; illustrated by Maryann Cocca-Leffler.
Whitman, 2002. ISBN: 0807508705. 32 pages.
Grades: 1–2.

Carlin is a raccoon who is afraid of everything. The bravest animal in the forest, the bear, is mixing up bravery soup, and he asks Carlin to get the missing ingredient from the monster's cave in the dark forest.

Support Materials for *The Bravest of Us All*

Reviews
- *Booklist*: May 1, 2000
- *Bulletin of the Center for Children's Books*: June, 2000

- *Children's Literature*: 2000
- *Horn Book*: Fall 2000
- *School Library Journal*: May 2000

3.3

Harry's Stormy Night by Una Leavy; illustrated by Peter Utton.
M. K. McElderry, 1995. ISBN: 0689506252. Unpaginated.
Grades: PreK–3.

Synopsis

During a power outage, Harry's family switches from electricity to candlelight. Harry learns that there are advantages to the problematic situation. Harry finds that instead of watching TV, he can draw pictures. His mom entertains him by telling stories of her childhood. By comforting his baby brother through the howling storm, Harry draws on new coping resources within himself and calms his own fears as well.

Booktalk

Outside, the wind whips up a storm. Can you hear it? Harry's mother warns him to come inside because "It's getting very wild." Dad says a tree fell down on some power lines and he expects a blackout. At first, when the lights go out, it is exciting. Mom makes the kitchen cozy, turning on a warm stove, filling a full tea kettle, and lighting candles that glow. She bakes an apple tart with the gas stove and Harry helps her make the pastry dough. He creates shadow puppets on the wall with his hands. Mom tells him stories about when she was a little girl. Later on in the stormy night, Harry gets into bed. The noises outside scare him. Shadows from the moon make him uncomfortable. The noise of the storm wakes up Harry's baby brother. Just as his mother made him feel safe with stories of her past, Harry tells baby Tom stories until he feels tired. Can you guess where Harry falls asleep that stormy night?

Shelf-Esteem Connection

Inner resources help a person cope and take control when the normal routine is disrupted.

THEME	MESSAGE	PLOT POINT CONNECTION	REINFORCING ACTIVITY	DISCUSSION QUESTIONS
Changing Your Attitude	There are ways to prepare for the unexpected, and sometimes bad situations bring out the best in people.	The storm causes the wind to howl and the downed power lines cause a blackout. Harry's mom does everything she can to make Harry feel comfortable: she bakes, she makes tea, and she lights candles. Throughout the storm Harry and his parents make the best of it.	Librarian: Shut the lights in the library (or classroom). Dramatize the story by using flashlights to help prepare students for a possible future power outage. Youngsters: Draw a picture of something you could do to help your family during a blackout.	What would make you feel more comfortable during a storm?

(Cont'd.)

THEME	MESSAGE	PLOT POINT CONNECTION	REINFORCING ACTIVITY	DISCUSSION QUESTIONS
Confidence	Being confident and self-assured when routines are threatened is crucial to clear thinking.	Mom tells stories of past blackouts. She knows that she has been through storms before, and she is confident she will get through storms again.	*Librarians:* Invite parents and teachers to tell stories of their memories of past blackouts. Supply the youngsters with either real pastry dough or Play-Doh and rolling pins to make a "pie" just like Harry does in the book. Then serve apple tarts for a snack for sensory connections.	What did Harry do to make him feel less afraid of the storm? What would you do?
Self-Reliance	Keep your wits about you and you will be able to make the best of a trying situation.	Having inner resources available helped Harry stay calm and entertained through the storm and helped him comfort his baby brother.	Ask students to write about how they could help someone else in case of a power outage.	Do you remember helping someone else and how you felt about yourself during that time?
Helping Others and Helping Yourself	When you are helpful to others you also help yourself.	When Harry felt afraid of the storm, he went into his brother's room. He sang to the baby, and he told him stories. Helping someone else made Harry less afraid.	Make up a story that you could tell to help someone cope with a storm.	How does helping someone else make you less afraid? Do you think of what you are trying to do instead of concentrating on your fear of the storm?

Book Hop

Franklin and the Thunderstorm by Paulette Bourgeois; illustrated by Brenda Clark.
Scholastic, 1998. ISBN: 0590026356. 29 pages.
Grades: PreK–2.
Franklin's friends help him overcome his fear of thunder and lightning by giving him funny explanations.

Classic Corner

There's a Nightmare in My Closet by Mercer Mayer; illustrated by Mercer Mayer.
Puffin, 1992. ISBN: 0140547126. 32 pages.
Grades: PreK–2.
A boy befriends his nightmares that are "hiding in his closet." He tucks his nightmare into bed and closes the closet door. By doing so, he shows the nightmare who is boss.

For Older Children

Explore different cultures' traditions with oral storytelling and explain how that method links generations of families together. This can begin a unit on folk tales or mythology.

Support Materials for *Harry's Stormy Night*

Awards and Honors
- *Smithsonian Magazine* Notable Books for Children: 1995
- *Baker & Taylor School Selection Guide K–8 Titles to Order*: 1997–98

Reviews
- *Booklist*: April 1, 1995
- *Horn Book*: Spring 1995
- *Publishers Weekly*: March 20, 1995
- *School Library Journal*: May 1, 1995

CHAPTER 4

Courage

4.1

Moses: When Harriet Tubman Led Her People to Freedom by Carole
Boston Weatherford; illustrated by Kadir Nelson.
Hyperion, 2006. ISBN: 0786851759. 42 pages.
Grades: K–3.

Synopsis

Through her fierce belief in her religion and her inner strength, Harriet Tubman became the
Moses of her people. She has the courage to leave her husband in the South and travel a rough
and harsh road to reach her promised land, Philadelphia, in the North. She feels the sun shine
down on her as she sees for the first time, the "free soil." She visits a station along the Underground Railroad as she passes on secret routes to freedom for runaway former slaves. Tubman
risks her life and her freedom to go back to the South to rescue her family.

Booktalk

How did Harriet Tubman lead her people to freedom? Harriet knew that slavery was wrong
and that she and her people were meant to be safe and free. She prayed that she would not be
caught as she made her way from the South to Philadelphia, where she would be a free
woman. But even when she made her way to the North, she still went back to the South to
find her family. She became a "conductor" of the Underground Railroad, which was not a
train, but a path toward a new life.

Shelf-Esteem Connection

Sometimes people take enormous risks to do what they know is right.

THEME	MESSAGE	PLOT POINT CONNECTION	REINFORCING ACTIVITY	DISCUSSION QUESTIONS
Relying on Inner Strength	Faith in oneself and knowledge of one's inner strength helps a	Harriet saw injustice in the South and tried to do what she could	Write down the signs Harriet received. Then tell how she reacted to	How did Harriet's inner goodness and strength help get

(Cont'd.)

THEME	MESSAGE	PLOT POINT CONNECTION	REINFORCING ACTIVITY	DISCUSSION QUESTIONS
Relying on Inner Strength *(Cont'd.)*	person get through hard times and perform difficult tasks.	to bring people to freedom.	them and what she did because of them.	her through difficult times?
Inspiration	Imagining oneself in the shoes of inspired people is a good way to feel inspired.	"Harriet, keep going. You have already glimpsed the future." This is one of the spiritual messages Harriet hears.	The message that Harriet heard kept her on the right path. Write or dictate a paragraph about a time when you thought you could not do something, but then with determination and inspiration, you were able to achieve at least part of your goal.	What positive words did Harriet hear? For example, keep going, no harm will come to you, use your gifts. What are other inspiring words you can think of to keep in the back of your mind?
Helping Others and Helping Ourselves	By learning about how other people cope with various challenges, it becomes possible to help them and oneself.	Harriet made 19 trips back to the South and she became a conductor on the Underground Railroad. She risked her life to save the lives of others. Harriet learned that by helping other slaves gain their freedom, she was doing her life's work.	Describe how Harriet's trips first helped others, which then led to her helping herself.	How does Harriet help this saying come to pass: "I mean for you to be free."
Communication	It is possible to communicate without speaking or writing a word.	The slaves used different ways to communicate via the Underground Railroad. One way was through the use of quilts that had secret messages woven into them.	Draw a picture of a quilt that would have a secret message from Harriet to one of the slaves back in the South.	How would an ex-slave listen or look for one of Harriet's messages?
Freedom	Freedom is so important to people that they will risk their lives to become free.	Harriet's one goal was to help her people become free men and women.	Write or dictate a paragraph or two about what you would miss for a day if you did not have your freedom.	What would you miss most if your freedoms were taken away? What would you try to gain back first when you became free?

Book Hop

A Picture Book of Harriet Tubman by David A. Adler; illustrated by Samuel Byrd.
Holiday House, 1992. ISBN: 0823409260. Unpaginated.
Grades: 2–4.
A clear, easy-to-read biography of the woman who helped hundreds of slaves escape in the 1850s.

Classic Corner

Harriet Tubman, a Woman of Courage by the editors of Time for Kids, with Renee Skelton.
HarperCollins, 2005. ISBN: 0060576081. 44 pages.
Grades: 2–5.
This biography of Harriet Tubman utilizes photographs from archives and an inspiring interview with Martin Luther King Jr.'s sister, Christine King Farris. There are also sidebars that provide more information about Tubman's life and legacy.

For Older Children

An Apple for Harriet Tubman by Glennette Tilley Turner; illustrated by Susan Keeter.
Albert Whitman, 2006. ISBN: 0807576433. Unpaginated.
Grades: 1–4.
To bring Harriet to life on a personal, understandable level, this book explains that Harriet worked in her master's apple orchard, but she was never allowed to eat the fruit. This was her favorite job as a child. Apples were a symbol of power and wealth to Harriet, and as soon as she became free, she bought a house in New York where she planted many apple trees.

Support Materials for *Moses: When Harriet Tubman Led Her People to Freedom*

Awards and Honors
• Caldecott Honor Book: 2006
• Coretta Scott King Award: 2006

Reviews
• *Kirkus*: September 1, 2006
• *School Library Journal*: October 1, 2006
• Reed Elsevier Inc., Starred Review: September 2006

4.2

A Picture Book of John F. Kennedy by David A. Adler;
illustrated by Robert Casilla.
Holiday House, 1991. ISBN: 0823408841. Unpaginated.
Grades: K–3.

Synopsis

Jack Kennedy was one of nine children born to Joseph and Rose Kennedy. When he was young, he was sickly, yet he was still able to be a serious student. He went to Harvard University, wrote a best-seller titled *Why England Slept*, and won a Navy medal for bravery during World War II. When his brother was killed in the war, he decided to enter politics, and he rose from being the Senator of Massachusetts to become President of the United States in 1960. Adler's book concentrates on Kennedy's days as a student and focuses on his achievements. On November 22, 1963, Kennedy was assassinated, an act that shocked the nation and the world. Illustrations cover major events in his life, starting with a family portrait and ending with John, Jr. saluting him during the funeral procession.

Booktalk

Do you think a boy who suffered from scarlet fever, whooping cough, and severe back trouble could grow up to be president of the United States? John F. Kennedy survived these serious illnesses and went on to graduate from Harvard University. He even wrote a famous book titled *Profiles in Courage*. (That book was published in a young reader's edition by Harper in 1961.) It featured biographies of famous men such as John Quincy Adams and Daniel Webster. During World War II he was considered a hero and the Navy awarded him a medal for bravery. A Japanese destroyer cut Kennedy's boat, the PT-109, in half. Kennedy rescued an injured sailor and swam for five hours, holding onto the man until both reached the shore safely. After the war, Kennedy ran for office and won the election to become the Senator of Massachusetts. In 1960, he became the youngest person to ever be elected President of the United States. When the President was killed on November 22, 1963, it shocked the nation.

Shelf-Esteem Connection

A good way to learn about courage is to study the lives of heroic people in history.

THEME	MESSAGE	PLOT POINT CONNECTION	REINFORCING ACTIVITY	DISCUSSION QUESTIONS
Persevering	You never know how far you can go until you try.	John F. Kennedy was sickly when he was young, but he still grew up to become president of the United States.	List the positive qualities that the young Kennedy possessed that helped make him a presidential hopeful in his adult years.	What facts do you know about President John F. Kennedy?
Education	Studying helps you reach your goals.	Kennedy knew that his studies were important, and he even worked hard to write a book of his own.	Draw a picture of what you want to be when you finish school.	Do you think Kennedy would have become president if he did not study and try to reach his goals?
Bravery	There are many things you can do to help others if you are brave.	When he was in the U.S. Navy, John Kennedy saved another person's life by swimming with him on his back for five hours. Kennedy won a Navy medal for his bravery.	Create a certificate that awards Kennedy an Honor for Bravery.	Do you know of someone else who won or could win an honor for bravery?

(Cont'd.)

THEME	MESSAGE	PLOT POINT CONNECTION	REINFORCING ACTIVITY	DISCUSSION QUESTIONS
Being Prepared	Preparation helps you to be successful in achieving your goals.	When Kennedy was on television, he appeared to be more relaxed and better prepared than his opponent, Richard Nixon, and he won the debates.	Write down one activity or event you prepared for and then list the results. For example, you practiced T-ball, and you scored a run. Or, you practiced piano and you played well at the recital.	The motto for the Boy Scouts is "Be Prepared." How do you come to the library (or to school) prepared each day?
Heroes	Reading about other people's heroic lives helps us in our own lives. We especially learn from those who overcome challenges.	John F. Kennedy was one of America's most beloved presidents. He was considered a real hero.	Read another biography about someone who is a hero in your eyes. It could be about a famous person, such as Helen Keller or Benjamin Franklin, or another president, such as Abraham Lincoln.	Who is a hero in your eyes? What is the difference between someone who is heroic versus someone who is famous (known for being known), such as a rock star, a sports figure, or an actor?

Book Hop

A Picture Book of Helen Keller by David A. Adler;
illustrated by John and Alexandra Wallner.
Holiday House, 1990. ISBN: 0823408183. Unpaginated.
Grades: K–3.
Hellen Keller overcame her handicaps of being blind and deaf.

How Ben Franklin Stole the Lightning by Rosalyn Schanzer.
HarperCollins, 2003. ISBN: 0688169937. Unpaginated.
Grades: K–2.
Ben Franklin is an inspiring figure who invented the lightning rod and many other objects we use daily.

Classic Corner

John F. Kennedy: A Photo-Illustrated Biography by Steve Potts.
Bridgestone, 1996. ISBN: 1560654546. 24 pages.
Grades: 1–4.

This book offers a more visual account of the life of John F. Kennedy. It covers events from his childhood, his service in the military and his subsequent ascent to the Presidency and later his assassination.

For Older Children

Activity: Create your own biography. Make up a small photo album about your "growing up" years. Include photographs and personal stories. Interview family members. Add letters you may have written or received, just as the author of this book included a telegraph that Jack Kennedy sent to his future wife, Jacqueline. Dictate captions for the photos. Show how far you have come from being a newborn baby to becoming a child going to school. Show how you could not walk or talk or read, but that now you can do all of those things.

Older children may also want to read:

John F. Kennedy; Thirty-fifth President of the United States by Zachary Kent.
Children's Press, 1987. ISBN: 0516013904. 99 pages.
Grades: 5 and up.

Kent tells the history of the president who left his mark on the civil rights movement, foreign relations, and exploration into outer space.

High Hopes: A Photobiography of John F. Kennedy by Deborah Heiligman.
National Geographic, 2003. ISBN: 0792261410. 63 pages.
Grades: 4–6.

A profile of President John F. Kennedy using large black-and-white photographs.

Support Materials for *A Picture Book of John F. Kennedy*

Reviews
• *Horn Book*: Spring 1991

CHAPTER 5

Emotions

5.1

Hooway for Wodney Wat by Helen Lester; illustrated by Lynn Munsinger.
Houghton Mifflin, 1999. ISBN: 0395923921. 32 pages.
Grades: PreK–3.

Synopsis
Rodney's classmates tease him because he can't pronounce his name. He has a speech impediment and cannot say the letter "R." Later Rodney becomes a hero when the same speech impediment drives away Camilla Capybara, the class bully.

Booktalk
Rodney the Rat has a big problem. He can't pronounce his Rs. All of his fellow rat classmates make fun of the way he talks. When everyone else has fun at recess, he is so embarrassed that he hides. What do you think happens to Rodney and the other rats when the enormous Camilla Capybara, a very big, mean, and clever rodent, joins the class? Rodney's speech mistakes turn the tables on Camilla and no one is afraid of her again. Now he is a hero!

Shelf-Esteem Connection
You cannot control the situation if people make fun of you or are even mean. You can learn to be prepared for attacks and learn not to repeat others' mistakes.

THEME	MESSAGE	PLOT POINT CONNECTION	REINFORCING ACTIVITY	DISCUSSION QUESTIONS
Humor	Word mistakes and word combinations can be funny. A good sense of humor can go a long way.	The rodents in this story have funny names, such as Minifeet Mouse and Grizzlefriz Guinea Pig.	Think of funny names for your pretend or real pet. Draw a picture of what this pet looks like.	Rodney was reading books with funny titles such as "Clear Squeaking" and "Squeak Up!" What are some other funny titles of books that Rodney could read?

(Cont'd.)

THEME	MESSAGE	PLOT POINT CONNECTION	REINFORCING ACTIVITY	DISCUSSION QUESTIONS
Laughing *with* People, Not *at* Them	It is fine to laugh together at a joke or when something is funny, but laughing at people is hurtful.	Camilla made all the rats feel uncomfortable. She laughs *at* Rodney.	Read comic strips and joke books to demonstrate how the class can laugh together at something that *is* funny.	As Rodney gains confidence, he pulls his head out of his jacket and his voice becomes stronger. What made his feelings change?
Making Mistakes	Everyone makes mistakes. This is inevitable. How a person handles the mistakes is what is important.	Characters in the book have trouble pronouncing words at times.	Look in the dictionary and try to pronounce a word with which you are unfamiliar.	Do you remember a time when you made a mistake and how you felt about it?
Body Language	Body language talks. It tells other people how a person is feeling.	When Rodney is ashamed and embarrassed, he pulls his jacket over his head just like a turtle. But when he is confident, he stands up straight and tall.	Draw a luncheon invitation for Rodney. Explain what you would serve him for lunch, and why you want to eat lunch with him. Now try to invite Rodney to lunch without saying any words.	How would you make sure Rodney is comfortable?
Heroes	Heroes are found in unlikely places. Sometimes the most unlikely person can be a hero.	Rodney puts the class bully in her place when playing a game of Simon Says.	Draw a picture or write about your hero in this story. Play a game of Simon Says.	How did Rodney become a hero? Why did telling Camilla Capybara to "Go West" win him respect? Who is one of your heroes at home or at the library?

Book Hop

All About Turtles by Jim Arnosky.
Scholastic, 2000. ISBN: 0590481495. 26 pages.
Grades: PreK–2.

When Rodney is criticized by the other children at recess, he hides inside his jacket the way a turtle pulls his head into his shell. This book has information about the physical characteristics, behavior, and survival techniques of different kinds of land and sea turtles.

Classic Corner

Did You Say Pears? by Arlene Alda.
Tundra, 2006. ISBN: 0887767397. 31 pages.
Grades: PreK–2.

Homonyms are words that sound alike and have the same spelling, but different meanings. Homophones are words that sound alike but are different in spelling and meaning. Arlene Alda's playful and very clever look at words puts together words and images in a book of photographs. A useful information page explaining the wordplay is included.

For Older Children

Make a list of words mispronounced in the book. Tell what they really should have said, such as Read the Sign instead of "Weed the Sign," Rake the Leaves instead of "Wake the leaves," and Go Rest, instead of "Go West." Then make up some more funny "wordplays" on your own.

Support Materials for *Hooway for Wodney Wat*

Awards and Honors

- American Library Association, Notable Books for Children: 2000
- Bank Street College of Education, *Best Children's Books of the Year*: 2000
- Children's ALA Notable Children's Books, Best Fiction: 2000
- Children's Blue Hen Award (Delaware), Best Fiction: 2000
- Children's Delaware Diamonds Primary (Grades K–2), Best Fiction: 2000
- Children's Flicker Tale Children's Book Award (North Dakota), Best Fiction: 2000
- Children's Picture Storybook Award (Georgia), Best Fiction: 2000
- Children's Picture Books (North Carolina), Best Fiction: 2000
- Children's Best-Parent's Choice Award—Gold Awards—Picture Book Category, Best Fiction: 1999
- School Library Journal Best Books, Best Fiction: 1999
- Virginia Reader's Choice Award—Primary School (Grades K–3), Best Fiction: 1999
- Beehive Awards (Utah)—Children's Picture Books, Best Fiction: 1999
- Blue Hen Book Award (Delaware), Best Fiction—Easy: 1999
- California Young Reader Medal—Primary, Best Fiction—Easy: 1999
- Delaware Diamonds—Primary (Grades K–2), Best Fiction—Easy: 1999
- Flicker Tale Children's Book Award, Best Fiction—Easy: 1999
- North Carolina Children's Book Award—Picture Books, Best Fiction—Easy: 1999
- Parent's Choice Award—Gold Awards, Best Fiction—Easy: 1999
- School Library Journal Best Books, Best Fiction—Easy: 1999
- Virginia Readers' Choice Award—Primary School (Grades K–3), Best Fiction—Easy: 1999

Reviews

- *Booklist*: May 1, 1999
- *Horn Book*: Fall 1999

5.2

Stand Tall, Molly Lou Melon by Patty Lovell; illustrated by David Catrow. G. P. Putnam's Sons, 2001. ISBN: 0399234160. Unpaginated. Grades: PreK–2.

Synopsis

Molly Lou Melon, the shortest girl in class, has buck teeth and a voice like a bullfrog. Her grandmother offers her sage advice: be proud of who she is and what she is, no matter what others might think. Her grandmother's advice really helps her when she moves to a new town and the bullies at her new school tease her.

Booktalk

How would you feel if you complained to your grandmother about being the shortest girl in your grade, and she told you to walk proudly so the world will look up to you? When Molly Lou Melon is sad about her buck teeth, her grandmother tells her to smile and the world will smile back. "Sing out clear and strong and the world will cry tears of joy" is grandmother's answer to the problem of Molly Lou's bullfrog voice. When she moves to a new town and starts a new school, bullies make fun of her physical attributes. Will Molly Lou take her grandmother's advice?

Shelf-Esteem Connection

If you believe in yourself, it does not matter what other people say.

THEME	MESSAGE	PLOT POINT CONNECTION	REINFORCING ACTIVITY	DISCUSSION QUESTIONS
Confidence	People should walk as proudly as they can, no matter how tall they are physically.	Molly Lou started going to a new school where the bully calls her ShrimpO. Remembering her grandmother's advice, Molly Lou stands tall, even though she is really quite short in stature.	Dramatize, role play, and take turns reading the parts of Molly Lou and her grandmother, so that everyone has a chance to empathize with Molly Lou. Then take a turn delivering grandma's advice. Write down how you would react if someone called you ShrimpO.	Can you think of a time when someone called you a name? How did you react? What can you do so that you are not insulted by what someone else calls you?
Humor	Even bullies respond to a big smile.	The bully calls Molly Lou "Bucky-Tooth Beaver," but Molly Lou learns that smiling can go a long way toward making new friends.	Molly Lou stacks pennies on her teeth just like a magic trick. Practice making stacks of items, such as blocks, or pennies. How high can you build that tower?	Discuss sayings such as "Sticks and stones may break my bones, but words will never harm me," and "Smile and the world smiles with you, frown and you frown alone."
Confidence	Don't be afraid to sing out clear and strong.	Even though she had a voice that sounded like a bullfrog, Molly Lou still sang out, loud and proud. In fact, she quacked so strongly that the bully had to go to the school nurse.	Draw the animal you would be if someone called you "buck-toothed." Would you look like a beaver? What if someone said you sounded like a sick duck when you sing? Cut out pictures from old wildlife magazines such as Ranger Rick or Your Big Backyard to show the animal you would represent and tell about the sound your animal would make.	Has anyone ever insulted your voice? What did you say back? What would you reply if you had thought about it ahead of time?

(Cont'd.)

THEME	MESSAGE	PLOT POINT CONNECTION	REINFORCING ACTIVITY	DISCUSSION QUESTIONS
Confidence	Believe in yourself and the world will believe in you, too.	Molly Lou is told that what she made in school was all wrong. Yet she showed confidence in what she did, and she wasn't afraid to try something new.	Think about a time when you felt bad about something you said, something you did, or something someone said about you. Write about how you could turn that negative comment around into something positive.	What do you think Molly Lou's grandmother might say to make her grandchild feel better?
Being Prepared	Having positive comments ready can help counter negative remarks.	Molly Lou has an appropriate positive response when someone puts her down.	Keep a chart of positive comments in the library and in the classroom. Help students remember and write down an arsenal of appropriate responses that can be utilized when negative incidents threaten their self-esteem. A newsletter including a list of positive responses can be sent home to be shared with parents.	Practice building positive responses to negative comments in the classroom, in the library, and at home.

Book Hop

Karate Girl by Mary Leary.
Farrar, Straus & Giroux, 2003. ISBN: 0374339775. Unpaginated.
Grades: K–2.

Mary learns karate and develops the inner confidence needed to stand up for herself and her little brother.

Classic Corner

Hazel's Amazing Mother by Rosemary Wells.
Dial, 1985. ISBN: 0803702108. 32 pages.
Grades: PreK–2.

Hazel's mother helps Hazel learn how to deal with bullies through the power of love. The strong bond between mother and child is exemplified. Hazel's mother becomes her daughter's heroine when she helps Hazel out of a difficult situation with some bullies.

For Older Children

It's Hot and Cold in Miami by Nicole Rubel.
Farrar, Straus & Giroux, 2006. ISBN: 0374336113. 202 pages.
Grades: 4–8.

Rachel has an identical twin and she is in constant competition with her. When her artistic talents are recognized, she feels special in her own way.

Support Materials for *Stand Tall, Molly Lou Melon*

Awards and Honors
- Arkansas Diamond Primary Book Award Winner: 2004
- *Books and More For Growing Minds*: 2001–2002
- Georgia Picture Book Award Nominee: 1997–98
- Nebraska Golden Sower Award Nominee, Grades K–3: 2003–04
- North Dakota Flicker Tale Picture Book Award Nominee: 2003–04

Reviews
- *Horn Book*: Spring 2002
- *Kirkus*: June 15, 2001
- *Publishers Weekly*: September 17, 2001
- *School Library Journal*: October 1, 2001
- *New York Times Book Review*: January 20, 2002

5.3

Whoa, Jealousy by Woodleigh Marx Hubbard with Madeline Houston.
G. P. Putnam's Sons, 2002. ISBN: 0399234357. 32 pages.
Grades: PreK–2.

Synopsis
All sorts of bad events begin to happen when jealousy, greed, envy, and rivalry take the form of various animals and invade a child's life. Jealousy is depicted as a mean, nasty chicken. Envy is a sneaky snake, Greed is a rude rat, and rivalry is an angry red hornet. The child must decide whether or not to let these demons into his life. It takes all his inner strength to triumph over these complicated negative emotions.

Booktalk
I bet many of you have said to your mom or dad, "It's not fair!" When the boy in our story says it, the color green surrounds him. Can you picture what it might be like if your emotions turned into real creatures and events? What would it look like if jealousy pecked at you like a chicken? What if envy really came to your home and "filled up your living room?" Now imagine if it could fill up the inner spaces in your heart in the same way. Suppose jealousy invited his next-door neighbors envy, greed, rivalry, and anger to help fill your inner space? What if envy turned into a snake? Or disrespect turned into a "rude rat?" What if rivalry could buzz in on hornet's wings and sting you? Is there any way you could stop them?

Shelf-Esteem Connection
It takes inner strength to triumph over jealousy, envy, greed, and rivalry.

THEME	MESSAGE	PLOT POINT CONNECTION	REINFORCING ACTIVITY	DISCUSSION QUESTIONS
Comparing Yourself to Others	When people compare themselves to others, they become dissatisfied and might even become green with envy.	The color green envelops the boy in the book as he complains: "It's not fair!"	Make stick puppets out of the chicken (jealousy), the snake (envy), the rat (greed), and the hornet (rivalry).	What happens to the narrator when he starts comparing himself to others? He thinks that Sallie is taller, Daniel is quicker, and Suzanne is cooler.
Being Strong	Keeping bad feelings out of one's life requires strength.	The narrator has to show strength not to let jealousy back into his life.	Re-enact the story using these stick puppets. Imitate the sounds each animal would make. For example, the chicken represents jealousy, the snake is envy, the rat is greed, and the hornet is rivalry.	How does "plucking the feathers of the chicken," "tying the snake in a knot," "trapping that rat," and "swatting the hornet" help the boy conquer these negative feelings?
Being Satisfied with What You Have	Those who are not satisfied with what they have will never be happy because they will always want more.	Greed, dressed up as a rat, lets the "gimmies" in, meaning "Gimme this" and "Gimme that."	Describe in a gratitude journal what you are thankful to have in your life.	What does the following statement mean: "Greed is never happy because it can NEVER get enough."
Sharing Feelings	Telling someone else how one feels makes it possible to let the feelings out instead of keeping them bottled up inside.	The boy has to tame the green envy snake and not listen when envy starts whispering in his ear. He needs to be happy with what he has, rather than letting jealousy take hold of him and his emotions. The boy has a choice to either succumb to these negative feelings or to recognize them, share them with others, and then refuse to allow them into his life.	Draw a picture of a friend, a teacher, or a buddy with whom you could share some of your feelings about being jealous or being greedy.	What would some of your feelings right now be like? Assign an animal to each one and a sound that it would make.

Book Hop

The Berenstain Bears Get the Gimmies by Stan and Jan Berenstain.
Random House, 1988. ISBN: 0394805666. 32 pages.
Grades: PreK–2.
Brother and Sister Bear find out what happens when they are greedy. They learn alternative ways to tame their greed and jealousy.

Classic Corner

Peter's Chair by Ezra Jack Keats,
HarperCollins, 1967. ISBN: 0060231114. Unpaginated.
Grades: PreK–2.

Peter has to adjust to many changes around his house when the new baby arrives. He must play quietly now, and he sees many of his baby furnishings being painted and given to his new sister Susie. He has to learn to manage his jealousy and to accept his new role as big brother.

For Older Children

Redirect your thoughts
When you know that jealousy, greed, or rivalry is hanging around you, redirect your thoughts toward gratitude, satisfaction, and contentment.

Divide a paper in half. On one side, write or draw a picture to illustrate one of the following negative thoughts: "Daniel is quicker" or "Suzanne is cooler," "Why can't I do that?" or "How come he got that?" Then, on the other half of the paper, write and draw what you can do faster than Daniel, or reasons why you are "cooler" than Suzanne.

How does thinking of what you *can* do feel better than dwelling on what you cannot do?

Support Materials for *Whoa, Jealousy*

Reviews
• *Horn Book*: Fall 2002
• *Kirkus*: June 1, 2002
• *Publishers Weekly*: June 10, 2002
• *School Library Journal*: July, 2002

5.4

Yesterday I Had the Blues by Jeron Ashford Frame;
illustrated by R. Gregory Christie.
Tricycle Press, 2003. ISBN: 1582460841. Unpaginated.
Grades: PreK–2.

Synopsis

A young boy copes with his own feelings and the ways his family experiences different emotions when he associates different colors to various moods. Every day brings new moods and new colors into focus.

Booktalk

Just imagine if you could color your day. Would you color "happy" yellow? Perhaps angry would be red. Is there a reason feeling sad is called "having the blues?" How about other members of your family? Your mom's moods would be different than your moods. Can you assign colors to their moods, too?

Shelf-Esteem Connection
Strong emotions are sometimes difficult to understand, especially for a young child. Associating colors with emotions is one way to deal with them in a more constructive way.

THEME	MESSAGE	PLOT POINT CONNECTION	REINFORCING ACTIVITY	DISCUSSION QUESTIONS
Feelings	Feelings are always changing.	The main character's feelings run the gamut of emotions and also the full spectrum of colors. The boy says he feels blue.	Remember that green is made up of the colors yellow and blue mixed together. Feelings are also made up of different emotions mixed together. Mix yellow paint (which is a sunny, uplifting color) with green paint (a soothing color) and see what shade you come up with on your painting. Then add some white paint to change a darker shade (a somber color) to a lighter color (a more soothing color).	What color would you assign to how you are feeling now?
Empathy	It is helpful to learn how to recognize other people's emotions. It makes it easier to deal with them.	The boy says he has the greens, Dad has the grays, Sasha has the pinks, and Talia has the indigos.	Write down the reasons for Dad's feeling "gray," Sasha's feeling "pink," and Talia's feeling "indigo."	Choose someone in your family—what color would you use to describe what you think he or she is feeling today?
Self-knowledge	Recognizing different feelings can help you identify your own moods and someone else's moods.	The boy finds music in the colors brought out by his variety of feelings.	Listen to various recordings, such as the sound of the saxophone to "hear the sound of indigo." It is the sound of jazz.	Can you label your moods or feelings using a color chart? Do you recognize when your moods or feelings change?
Expressing Emotion through Art	Art and music are helpful in working through tough emotions because they provide an outlet for expressing feelings.	Gram's got the yellows and Mama has the reds. These are bright, sometimes fierce colors.	Try describing how you are feeling using colors. Use magic markers, crayons, or paints to keep track of how you feel and why you feel that way.	Create a mural to show that your group is a rainbow of colors that changes each day.

(Cont'd.)

THEME	MESSAGE	PLOT POINT CONNECTION	REINFORCING ACTIVITY	DISCUSSION QUESTIONS
Communicating in Different Ways	There are different ways to communicate feelings without using words.	The narrator of the book describes his family's feelings through the use of colors.	Create a booklet of emotions and draw the corresponding color for each on the opposite page. Then write down the reasons why you think someone would be feeling that way (e.g. happy, angry, excited, mad).	What are some important ways you can use to share your feelings?

Book Hop

When Sophie Gets Angry—Really, Really Angry by Molly Bang.
Blue Sky Press, 1999. ISBN: 0590189794. Unpaginated.
Grades: PreK–2.

Sophie gets really angry; she kicks, screams, roars, runs, and sometimes cries. But when she notices the world around her—rocks, trees, water, birds, the wind in her hair—she cools down and returns to her family.

Classic Corner

Alexander and the Terrible, Horrible, No Good, Very Bad Day by Judith Viorst;
illustrated by Ray Cruz.
Aladdin, 1987. ISBN: 0689711735. 32 pages.
Grades: PreK–2.

Some days seem to go from bad to worse. How does Alexander handle things when he wakes up with gum in his hair, he trips over his skateboard, he drops his sweater in the sink, his mother forgets to put dessert in his lunch, and his dentist finds a cavity? He thinks about moving to Australia, but he goes to bed with the conviction that tomorrow will be a better day.

For Older Children

Judy Moody by Megan McDonald; illustrated by Peter Reynolds.
Candlewick, 2000. ISBN: 0763606855. 160 pages.
Grades: 2–4.

Judy Moody is in a bad mood and is very grumpy when she begins a new school year.

Support Materials for *Yesterday I Had the Blues*

Awards and Honors
• *Bulletin of the Center for Children's Books*, Blue Ribbon Award: 2003
• Georgia Children's Book Award Nominees: 2003–04
• North Carolina Children's Book Award Nominee: 2004–05
• Charlotte Zolotow Award, Highly Commended: 2004
• Ezra Jack Keats New Writer and New Illustrator Award: 2004

Reviews
- *Booklist*: November 1, 2003
- *Horn Book*: Spring 2004
- *Kirkus*: August 15, 2003
- *Multicultural Review*: March 2004
- *Publishers Weekly*: September 15, 2003
- *School Library Journal*: October 1, 2003

5.5

You Can Do It, Sam by Amy Hest; illustrated by Anita Jeram.
Candlewick, 2003. ISBN: 0763619345. Unpaginated.
Grades: PreK–2.

Synopsis
Sam, a young bear, gains confidence when he successfully delivers mother's cakes—all by himself—through the snow.

Booktalk
Close your eyes, take a deep breath, and you can almost smell the delicious cakes that Mrs. Bear and her son Sam are baking for all of their friends on Plum Street. Sam agrees to safely deliver all of his mother's cakes, even though a snowstorm will make it difficult. Finally, they are ready to be packed up and delivered. He isn't sure if he can make the deliveries. What do you think will happen to Sam and the freshly baked cakes?

Shelf-Esteem Connection
Even though a task seems insurmountable, with persistence and small steps, it can be accomplished.

THEME	MESSAGE	PLOT POINT CONNECTION	REINFORCING ACTIVITY	DISCUSSION QUESTIONS
Confidence	What seems impossible becomes possible by taking small steps and having self-confidence.	The snow makes it very difficult to deliver the cakes that Mrs. Bear and her son bake. Sam believes in his ability to make the deliveries and one step at a time, he is able to go from neighbor to neighbor.	*Librarian:* Write down a recipe for muffins. Discuss the ingredients. Send home a copy of the recipe for home use.	Think of something you can do now that you could not have done a year ago.
Bravery	In order to succeed a person has to be brave enough to believe in him- or herself.	Sam makes the deliveries even though he initially thought the snow would make it impossible.	Make a list of what you have done that you initially thought you would not be able to do.	What have you done now by yourself that you learned to do in small steps, such as doing math problems or tying your shoe?

(Cont'd.)

THEME	MESSAGE	PLOT POINT CONNECTION	REINFORCING ACTIVITY	DISCUSSION QUESTIONS
Perseverance	One should not give up trying just because a task seems very difficult. Have confidence, keep trying, and take small steps.	Sam wasn't certain that he could do what he first set out to accomplish. But he did it, one step at a time.	*Librarian:* If your class decides to bake muffins, the students may make deliveries like Sam does. In a school, include various members of the staff, such as the principal, the nurse, and the office staff. In a public library, include the staff.	What would you like to learn how to do, and how would learning it in small parts make it easier to accomplish?
Generosity	Being generous with others can make a person feel proud and happy.	Sam and his mother deliver their baked goods with an outstretched arm and a kind heart.	Gift-wrap a book which you would like to give to someone else in the class.	Can you remember giving something to someone else and how glad it made them feel and how proud it made you feel?

Book Hop

I Can Do It Too! by Karen Baicker; illustrated by Ken Wilson-Max.
Handprint Books, 2003. ISBN: 1929766831. Unpaginated.
Grades: PreK–1.

A young African-American girl builds confidence in her abilities as she models the efforts of her family members. This girl wants to pour juice like her dad does, she wants to put on clothing just like her older sister, and she wants to read a book just like her grandfather.

Classic Corner

The Runaway Bunny by Margaret Wise Brown; illustrated by Clement Hurd.
Harper & Row, 1972 (originally published in 1942). ISBN: 0060207653. Unpaginated.
Grades: PreK–2.

A young bunny tries to exercise his independence from his mother. He is able to spread his wings because his mother's unconditional love is always there to support him.

For Older Children

Rehearsal for the Bigtime by Berniece Rabe.
Franklin Watts, 1988. ISBN: 0531105040. 144 pages.
Grades: 4–6.

Margo is an 11-year-old who learns that by practicing on her instrument she can build her confidence and gain admiration from her friends and family.

Support Materials for *You Can Do It, Sam*

Awards and Honors
- Bistro Book of the Year Award Merit Award (Ireland): 2003–04
- Texas Children's Round Table, Two By Two Reading List, Grades: PreK–2: 2002

Reviews
- *Booklist*: November 11, 2003
- *Horn Book*: Spring 2004
- *Kirkus*: October 1, 2003
- *School Library Journal*: October 1, 2003

CHAPTER 6

Moving

6.1

I'm Not Moving, Mama! by Nancy White Carlstrom;
illustrated by Thor Wickstrom.
Macmillan, 1990. ISBN: 0027172864. 32 pages.
Grades: PreK–3.

Synopsis
A young mouse and his mama talk about moving to a new home. At first the youngster resists, but finally he learns that as long as he is with his family, he can remember the old place while learning to adjust to the new one. Mouse finally realizes that being together with his family is what really matters, not their address.

Booktalk
A young mouse is full of bitter feelings when he finds out his family is moving to a new home. His mama must convince him to look forward to the move. She tells him that the sun will still shine at his new address, he will find a new favorite hiding place, and there will be another mirror. Mama tells her son that he is needed in his new home. Otherwise, who will make funny faces in that mirror? Mouse tells him he can pack all of his important stuff: the building blocks, the green dinosaur, and his two-wheeler. As the move approaches, he still refuses to go! She tells him: "We'll remember the star window and the climbing tree, the long rope swing and the sunset seat. Someday, we'll say, 'Remember how good it was to live in that old place?'" Do you think mouse will join his family in the move to their new home? What would you do?

Shelf-Esteem Connection
When you move to a new house, you take all of the important things with you, especially your memories.

THEME	MESSAGE	PLOT POINT CONNECTION	REINFORCING ACTIVITY	DISCUSSION QUESTIONS
Self-identity	People take themselves wherever they go. They might change location, but they are still the same inside.	Mouse makes a complete list of things that are important to him that should be moved to the new house. But Mama reassures him that what is most important is that he will still be the same Mouse, and she needs him to be happy.	Decide what you would bring to your new house if you were moving. Make or dictate a list. Then draw these items or cut out pictures from old magazines to show what you want to pack and what can be left behind. Make a collage of the items you want to bring.	What is the most important thing you would bring to your new home?
Family Love	Being together is more important than where people are located.	Mouse agrees it is better to stay all together as a family in a new place than to stay all alone in the old place.	List the reasons Mama gives to Mouse to explain how he is needed more than ever in their new home.	Whom would you wish to spend time with at a new house or at an old house? Why?
Helping One Another	Help (and a sense of humor) is needed when a family moves.	Mama convinces her son that he is needed at the new address because he needs to make funny faces in the mirror and paint the clouds pink. She would miss that if he weren't there.	Draw a picture of Mouse making funny faces in the mirror or painting the clouds pink.	How would you help out if your family moved to a new home?
Focusing on Positives	Even things that seem totally negative have some positive aspects.	Mama convinces Mouse that the sun will still be shining at this new house, he will find a new favorite hiding place, and there will be another mirror in which he can make funny faces.	Divide a paper in half. On one half, draw some positive feelings that Mouse has about his old house, such as knowing a good hiding spot, the mirror, the sunshine, or the star window. On the other half of the paper, draw some positives about the new house, such as making new friends, being together with the family, and finding a new hiding spot.	Think of one negative thought you would have about moving. How could you turn it into something positive?
Keeping Memories Alive	Remembering things means they are present in your mind.	Mouse will always be able to remember the place he lived before: the star window, the climbing tree, the rope swing, the sunset seat.	Play a memory game called: "I am Moving to a New House . . . and I am Going to Bring____." Each child may add one item to the list, but must repeat the prior participants' entries. The last person should try to recite all of the items.	What memory do you have that you would you like to share?

Book Hop

Ira Says Goodbye by Bernard Waber.
Houghton Mifflin, 1988. ISBN: 0395483158. 38 pages.
Grades: PreK–2.
Ira comes to terms with his best friend Reggie's enthusiasm about moving to a new place.

Classic Corner

Gila Monsters Meet You at the Airport by Marjorie Weinman Sharmat;
illustrated by Byron Barton.
Macmillan, 1980. ISBN: 0027824500. 32 pages.
Grades: PreK–2.
A New York City boy's preconceived ideas of life in the West make him very apprehensive about the family's move there.

For Older Children

Home Is East by Many Ly.
Delacorte, 2005. ISBN: 0385732228. 294 pages.
Grades: 4–8.
After her mother moves out, a ten-year-old Cambodian–American girl and her old-fashioned father leave their home in Florida to begin a new life in San Diego, experiencing turmoil and change as they slowly adjust to their new circumstances.

Support Materials for *I'm Not Moving, Mama!*

Awards and Honors
• *Best Books for Children*, 6th edition: 1998
• *Picture Books to Enhance the Curriculum*: 1996

Reviews
• *Horn Book*: Spring 1990
• *Publishers Weekly*: November 15, 1999

6.2

A Packet of Seeds by Deborah Hopkinson; illustrated by Bethanne Andersen.
Greenwillow, 2004. ISBN: 0060090898. Unpaginated.
Grades: K–5.

Synopsis

A nineteenth-century pioneer family moves west. The father is eager and loves a new adventure. The mother is full of sorrow and misses the home she left. Mother is so sad that she will not even name her new baby daughter until her older daughter, Annie, thinks of just the right thing to cheer her up.

Booktalk

How hard do you think it was for a family to move to a new life in the American West during the nineteenth century? Annie, the daughter, narrates this insightful, exciting story of how her parents greeted the challenge in opposite ways. Papa is eager to join the adventure—to be part of the pioneer movement, populated by brave and strong people. Mama does not want to leave her home. Annie says, "All Pa could see was the new land before him. All Momma could feel was the sorrow of leaving everything behind." Annie worries that her mother's sadness will never cease and wonders if she will ever smile again. Annie's mother is so sad that when the new baby is born, Momma is afraid she will not live and does not even give her a name. Will they ever name the baby? What will they call her? Will Momma ever get well and adjust to her new home? Is there anything Annie can do to help?

Shelf-Esteem Connection

There are positive and negative emotions that arise when a family moves. Exploring these emotions helps verbal and nonverbal expressions of the feelings of displacement, anticipation, and fear of the unknown. The important point is that everyone in the family must maintain a positive attitude.

THEME	MESSAGE	PLOT POINT CONNECTION	REINFORCING ACTIVITY	DISCUSSION QUESTIONS
Changing How You Look at Life	Looking at something frightening very carefully may unearth things that are really likeable.	Annie is fearful of the coyotes, but then she finds out that their songs are welcome sounds on the prairie. Momma mostly slept and stayed in bed, but then she offered to plant the daisy, larkspur, morning glory, poppy, and hollyhock seeds.	Turn something potentially fearful into something understandable by changing your viewpoint. On half of a piece of paper, draw a picture of something you find fearsome. Then, on the other half of the paper, draw it so it looks different. It could be funny, colorful, or silly.	How did Annie overcome her fear of the coyotes? Were you ever afraid of a particular animal? What did you do to overcome that fear?
Positives and Negatives	There are pluses and minuses about moving to a new home.	Momma misses her old home because she had a fine house, dear friends, and a garden.	Make a plus column and a minus column for the positives and negatives about the family's move out west.	Did you ever need help making an important decision? Can you think of something that was negative at first, but then turned into a positive?
Persistence	Persistence and a positive attitude help a person reach his or her goals.	The settlers were determined to make a home in the West. Although the ground was too hard to dig up, Annie persisted in swinging a hatchet in the ground, and eventually the earth was ready for planting.	Draw a picture of something you were not able to do before this year, but through hard work and repeated attempts, you are able to do it today. (For example, it could be playing T-ball, or soccer, or perhaps dancing.)	What steps did you have to follow to be successful at something that was hard to do, such as learning to play a musical instrument?

(Cont'd.)

THEME	MESSAGE	PLOT POINT CONNECTION	REINFORCING ACTIVITY	DISCUSSION QUESTIONS
Carrying Seeds	There is a double meaning to the carrying of seeds. It can refer to a packet of seeds for planting or it can refer the beginnings of who a person is; the person's roots. All people carry the seeds of who they are wherever they go.	The word *seed* reminds the reader of the packet of seeds that Momma's friends have to give her, but also to Momma's roots.	*Librarian:* Buy seed packets for the group and distribute them. The children could plant flowers and vegetable seeds just as the characters in the book do. Children may bring their plants home so they can tell their families the significance of the plantings and the tie-in to the book.	How will you care for your seedlings? What will you need to do to help them to grow?
Adjusting to Change	Adjusting to change makes it possible to carry out the normal parts of living once again.	Momma decides to name the baby Janice Rose. The name is dedicated to Momma's sister and to the prairie roses planted in the new home. This is one signal that Momma has adjusted to the move.	Write or dictate a letter to a family member who has moved away and tell him or her about Momma's adjustment to her new life.	If you have moved to a new home, how did you make the adjustment? What was hard about leaving your old neighborhood? What reminders could you bring with you? What did you have to leave behind?

Book Hop

The Carrot Seed by Ruth Krauss; illustrated by Crockett Johnson.
Harper Trophy, 2004. 60th Anniversary Edition. ISBN: 0064432106. Unpaginated.
Grades: K–1.

This classic book portrays the simple determination and the slow and steady process of caring for and watching seeds as they grow to bear fruit—or in this case, carrots. The children could dramatize this book as a short play.

Classic Corner

Words West: Voices of Young Pioneers by Ginger Wadsworth.
Clarion, 2003. ISBN: 0618234756. 191 pages.
Grades: 2–5.

This nonfiction book about pioneers moving westward tells the stories of young pioneers through their letters, diaries, and journals.

For Older Children

Writing exploration
What is the meaning of the expression "We carry the seeds of who we are wherever we go"?
Use this topic as a writing prompt.

Support Materials for *A Packet of Seeds*

Awards and Honors
• Choices, Cooperative Children's Book Center: 2005
• Arkansas Diamond Primary Book Award Nominee, Grades K–3: 2003–04
• Nebraska Golden Sower Award Nominee, Grades K–3: 2003–04

Reviews
• *Booklist*: May 15, 2004
• *Horn Book*: Fall 2004
• *Kirkus*, Book Review Stars: March 1, 2004
• *Library Media Connection*: January 2005
• *School Library Journal*: April 1, 2004

6.3

Why Did We Have to Move Here? by Sally J. K. Davies.
Carolrhoda, 1997. ISBN: 1575050463. Unpaginated.
Grades: PreK–3.

Synopsis

William is having difficulty learning to live in his new home and adjusting to his new school until he decides that with a little effort he can make new friends.

Booktalk

William is awfully upset about moving away from everything that is familiar and starting from scratch. Imagine moving to a new place, going to a new school, and trying to make all new friends. In the wintertime, he comes up with a great idea that suddenly makes everyone want to be his friend. Find out how he turned his problems to his advantage.

Shelf-Esteem Connection

Moving to a new home brings changes in the routine, but thinking of it as an opportunity makes it easier to adjust.

THEME	MESSAGE	PLOT POINT CONNECTION	REINFORCING ACTIVITY	DISCUSSION QUESTIONS
Patience	It is difficult to find important items right away after a move. Packing special things in a box and marking it clearly will help ease frustrations.	William feels frustrated when he cannot locate what he wants when he needs it because he is now forced to share a room with his brother.	*Librarian:* Play a game with the group. Half of the children may pack a box, and the other half may use clues to guess what is inside of the box. Practice packing and unpacking a real suitcase with items the children can bring to the library.	What do you do when you feel frustrated by something or someone?

(Cont'd.)

THEME	MESSAGE	PLOT POINT CONNECTION	REINFORCING ACTIVITY	DISCUSSION QUESTIONS
Humor	Finding the humor in a situation helps to ease the tension.	Everyone stares at William when he wears his coat and boots because it wasn't appropriate attire, but it was the only option available to him.	Write or dictate a funny story about wearing an old winter coat and leaky boots to school.	Have you ever had to wear something different to school than what you wanted to wear because your choice was misplaced or was in the laundry? How did you feel?
Books as Friends	Books can go wherever a person may move. They are treasured, familiar friends.	When William is at school, you can read the titles of the books on his desk: *Wild Science Facts* and *Flight Path*.	Write down or draw a picture of what William is interested in reading about. Now write down what you are interested in reading about.	What do you think William was learning about at school that day? Can you name one science fact you would like to share with William?
Cooperation	Often it is possible to learn more by cooperating with others than by always working alone.	The twins were partners in a science project called Our Plant Grows.	Draw a picture of the seeds, the earth, the planting procedure, and write down what you would need to do to keep that plant growing (For example, watering the plant, sunshine).	Can you remember a time when you worked on a project with someone else? Did it turn out better than if you would have worked on it all by yourself?
Making New Friends	Sometimes it takes some ingenuity to make new friends at a new school.	The teacher asked Peter to give William a tour of the school. This gave William a chance to make a new friend as well as learn about the school.	Pretend you are going to give William a tour of your school or library Write down what you would want to show him and why.	What are some ways William make new friends?

Book Hop

The Lost and Found House by Michael Cadnum;
illustrated by Steve Johnson and Lou Fancher.
Viking, 1997. ISBN: 0670848840. Unpaginated.
Grades: K–3.

A young boy leaves his old house wistfully and welcomes his new house with measured optimism and hopefulness.

Classic Corner

The Town Mouse and the Country Mouse retold by Ellen Schecter;
illustrated by Holly Hannon.
Gareth Stevens, 1996. ISBN: 0836816226. 47 pages.
Grades: K–2.

Town Mouse and Country Mouse discover what it is like to live in the place where they think the grass is always greener.

For Older Children

Making new friends

Everyone appreciates William's idea to skate on the frozen tennis court. William realizes that his old friends were new at one time, too. He is on his way toward making new friends. Write down what the words to the well-known song "Make New Friends, but Keep the Old" mean to you.

Support Materials for *Why Did We Have to Move Here?*

Awards and Honors
- *Children's Literature* Choice List: 1998
- *Best Books for Children*, 6th and 7th editions: 1998, 2002
- *Baker & Taylor School Selection Guide K–8 Titles to Order*: 1998–99.

Reviews
- *Booklist*: December, 1997
- *Horn Book*: Spring 1998
- *Kirkus*: October 15, 1997

CHAPTER 7

New Sibling

7.1

The Baby Sister by Tomie dePaola.
G. P. Putnam's Sons, 1996. ISBN: 0399229086. Unpaginated.
Grades: PreK–2.

Synopsis

Tommy looks forward to the arrival of the newest family member. He hopes his mother will give him a baby sister "with a red ribbon in her hair." But when his mother is in the hospital, Tommy has to adjust to staying at home with his strict grandmother, Nana Fall-River.

Booktalk

Do you have a large or a small family? Tommy is a member of a very large family, with lots of aunts, uncles, and cousins. One day Tommy finds out that his family is going to get bigger by one—a new baby! He is very excited about this upcoming event and asks his mother if the new baby can be a girl, "with a red ribbon in her hair." Tommy balances the excitement of the new baby with the worry over what it will be like to have his strict grandmother take care of him until his mother and the new baby come home. Has anyone become a new older brother or sister? Did you feel like Tommy or did you feel differently?

Shelf-Esteem Connection

With preparation, an older sibling can feel comfortable in the new role of big brother or big sister.

THEME	MESSAGE	PLOT POINT CONNECTION	REINFORCING ACTIVITY	DISCUSSION QUESTIONS
Change	Nothing stays the same forever. Change is inevitable.	The family starts to get ready for the new baby's arrival by painting the nursery, getting a crib and changing table, and hanging new curtains.	Draw a picture of other things the family needs to do to get ready for the new baby. (For example, buy bottles, diapers, and baby clothes).	What has been your experience in waiting for a new baby?

(Cont'd.)

THEME	MESSAGE	PLOT POINT CONNECTION	REINFORCING ACTIVITY	DISCUSSION QUESTIONS
Adjusting to Change	Having a positive attitude makes change easier to adjust to in any situation.	Tommy wants to be included in all the changes, so he paints a picture to put on the wall of the nursery.	Write about how you, as a big brother or sister, could help out at home to prepare for a new baby's arrival. If you don't have a baby sister or brother, just think of a baby cousin or make believe you have one.	How have you been able to help out at home as a new big brother or big sister? Or perhaps you have helped with another child.
Being Part of a Family	There are special aspects of being a big brother or sister and also tasks we must take care of while we try to do our part.	Tommy gets to feel the baby kicking in his mother's tummy. He looks forward to staying with his Aunt Nell when mom has to go to the hospital. But things don't work out exactly as planned. Aunt Nell does not come to stay with Tommy, as he had hoped.	If you were in Tommy's place, who would you choose to be the new "babysitter"? Write down what time the sitter will come over to your house, and make a list of games you would like to play with him or her.	How could you welcome a new member of your family?
Sharing and Caring	Children like to show their affection for their new siblings.	Tommy wants to show his affection for his new sibling. He gets to hold his new sister Maureen in his arms and this makes him very happy.	Pretend you are making preparations for the new baby's arrival. Just as Tommy drew a picture for the new baby's room, ask children to make a drawing for a new baby's room. Librarian: Older children could write a poem or a story for the new baby. Creating something for the new baby will help with the bonding process.	How do you show you care for your baby brother or sister?
Family Love	Parents' love for their children is constant. Even when parents go away, they love their children and will come back.	As soon as mom returned from the hospital, she asked to see Tommy right away.	Plan a dinner to eat with your baby sister or brother or your grandmother. Cut out pictures from old magazines of some of your favorite foods and make a food collage.	Can you remember a special meal you had with a family member? Why was it special? What did you eat?

Book Hop

Dear Baby: Letters from Your Big Brother by Sarah Sullivan; illustrated by Paul Meisel. Candlewick, 2005. ISBN: 0763621269. Unpaginated.
Grades: PreK–2.

Mike writes letters to his baby sister before she is even born, describing what he thinks it will be like to be her older brother.

Classic Corner

When the New Baby Comes, I'm Moving Out by Martha G. Alexander.
Dial, 1981. ISBN: 0803795637. 32 pages.
Grades: PreK–2.

Oliver does not like the idea of becoming a big brother. In terms clearly reminiscent of Peter in Ezra Jack Keats' *Peter's Chair*, Oliver balks when his highchair and crib are being painted to make way for his new sibling.

A Baby Sister for Frances by Russell Hoban; illustrated by Lillian Hoban.
HarperCollins: 1993. ISBN: 0060223359. 27 pages.
Grades: PreK–2.

This classic story of sibling adjustment shows how Frances copes with a newly enlarged family. Her rhyming songs show her progress from jealousy to love and, finally, to acceptance of her new sibling.

For Older Children

This book is told in rhyme. Ask the students to listen to these rhyming words from the book and repeat the sounds: dad-had, got-lot, way-they, humming-coming, joy-boy, care-share, another-brother, hair-share. Then take your rhyming words and make up and illustrate your own book or poem for the new baby.

Support Materials for *The Baby Sister*

Awards and Honors
• Michigan Reader's Choice Award Nominee: 2000

Reviews
• *Booklist*: March 15, 1996
• *Kirkus*: February 15, 1996
• *Publishers Weekly*: February 19, 1996

7.2

Sophie and the New Baby by Laurence Anholt; illustrated by Catherine Anholt.
Albert A. Whitman, 2000. ISBN: 080757550X. Unpaginated.
Grades: PreK–2.

Synopsis

Sophie is very happy to play with her dolls until she finds out that she will be joined by a brother or sister during the winter months. She goes through the seasons wondering what it will be like to have a new baby in the family. When her brother arrives in the wintertime, Sophie isn't so sure she wants him to stay. Finally she accepts her position as the big sister in the family and rejoices in playing with her new baby brother.

Booktalk

Imagine what it would be like to wait through the seasons of the year for a new baby brother or sister. Going through spring, summer, fall, and then finally reaching winter will seem like a very long time. But when the time finally comes, will Sophie be ready for her new position as big sister in the family? Will she be ready to share with the new baby—especially, will she be ready to share her parents' time?

Shelf-Esteem Connection

When a new baby arrives on the scene, the first child must make many adjustments and sometimes may not want to make those changes. But eventually, change brings growth to all members of the family.

THEME	MESSAGE	PLOT POINT CONNECTION	REINFORCING ACTIVITY	DISCUSSION QUESTIONS
Passage of Time	Young children's perception of time can be measured by the changing of the seasons.	Sophie is told by her parents that her brother or sister will be a winter baby.	Work with a calendar to separate the months that comprise spring, summer, fall, and winter.	What activities do you look forward to doing in the spring? What about summer? What happens in the fall? What is special about the wintertime for you?
Change	Children are often resistant to the changes that a new baby brings.	Sophie learns that being a big sister brings responsibilities as well as privileges. She also learns that the baby is with the family to stay and that she can't take the baby back.	Make a list of tasks (and fun things, too) that Sophie could undertake to help the family with their new baby. Draw a picture of Sophie playing with the new baby.	What could you do at home to help out if your family had a new baby or a new pet?
Coping with Anger	There are many ways to deal with anger. Some are better than others.	Sophie cries because her world has changed so much.	Write down what other ways Sophie could have gotten her feelings off her chest. Could she have written a poem? Could she have drawn a picture? Could she have talked to someone else?	It took a long time for Sophie to get used to the Winter Baby. How do you think Sophie could have gotten used to him more quickly? Could she have played with him more?
Teaching New Skills	Having a new baby in the family teaches an older child how to become more grown up. The older child can also help teach the baby important skills.	The baby made happy noises when Sophie played with him. That made Sophie feel really good.	Make a list of the things that the baby taught Sophie (patience, for example) and what Sophie taught the baby (how to go for a walk in his carriage).	What new things would you be able to teach a baby? For example, when you read to a baby, you help him or her learn to talk.

(Cont'd.)

THEME	MESSAGE	PLOT POINT CONNECTION	REINFORCING ACTIVITY	DISCUSSION QUESTIONS
Patience	Children have to learn patience because there are going to be times when they have to wait a long time for something or when someone else's needs need to come first.	Sophie didn't like the fact that the baby needed to be fed and changed with immediacy.	Sophie loses her patience with her brother and wants to take him back. She learns that he is there to stay. Write the baby brother a note telling him why you would want him to stay if you were Sophie. For example, you might want to play with him, he smells good, and you like to give him kisses.	How have you learned patience during this school year? Did you have to wait your turn? Did you have to share? Did you have to wait to get the librarian's attention?

Book Hop

Everett Anderson's Nine Month Long by Lucille Clifton; illustrated by Ann Grifalconi.
Rinehart and Winston, 1978. ISBN: 0030435366. 31 pages.
Grades: PreK–2.
Everett Anderson's mom remarries and tells him that she is expecting a new baby. Everett adjusts to the idea over the course of the pregnancy, deciding that there is enough love to share with an addition to the family. He is disappointed, though, that Mom can hardly run now and has to rest quite often.

Classic Corner

She Come Bringing Me That Little Baby Girl by Eloise Greenfield;
illustrated by John Steptoe.
J. B. Lippincott, 1974. ISBN: 0397315864. 32 pages.
Grades: PreK–2.
Kevin has difficulty adjusting to a new baby at home until he embraces his role as a big brother.

For Older Children

Waiting for Gregory by Kimberly Willis Holt; illustrated by Gabi Swiatkowska.
Henry Holt, 2006. ISBN: 0805073884. Unpaginated.
Grades: K–2.
This book is likened to a "show waiting to begin." A young girl awaits the arrival of her new baby cousin, who causes all kinds of excitement and anticipatory delight.

Support Materials for *Sophie and the New Baby*

Awards and Honors
• Best Books: Smithsonian Magazine's Notable Books for Children: 2000.

Reviews
- *Booklist*: September 15, 2000
- *Cooperative Children's Book Center Choices*: 2001
- *Horn Book Guide*: Spring 2001
- *Kirkus*: October 1, 2000
- *Lorgnette-Heart of Texas Reviews*: Volume 13, No. 4

CHAPTER **8**

Multiculturalism

8.1

Abuela by Arthur Dorros; illustrated by Elisa Kleven.
Dutton, 1991. ISBN: 0525447504. Unpaginated.
Grades: PreK–2.

Synopsis
While riding on a bus with her grandmother, a young Latina girl imagines that they are carried up into the sky and fly over New York City. Many Spanish phrases are included in the text.

Booktalk
Imagine that you could take your favorite relative and pretend to fly over your city or town. What would you see? What would look different from high above the clouds? This girl and her loving grandmother take a trip high above New York (without an airplane) to view the Statue of Liberty and even their own neighborhood.

Shelf-Esteem Connection
Imagination can take a child many places, especially when a loved one comes along on the journey.

THEME	MESSAGE	PLOT POINT CONNECTION	REINFORCING ACTIVITY	DISCUSSION QUESTIONS
Relationships with Grandparents	The relationship between a grandchild and grandparent is a special kind of love.	Abuela and her granddaughter share a special relationship. They spend a lot of time together and share a lot of love.	Write down some fun activities you would like to do with a special relative.	Why would you want to do those things? Are they things you both enjoy doing? What could you learn to do from your special relative?

(Cont'd.)

THEME	MESSAGE	PLOT POINT CONNECTION	REINFORCING ACTIVITY	DISCUSSION QUESTIONS
Reality and Imagination	Stories often have a mixture of reality and imagination.	Abuela takes her granddaughter to the park. That is a real trip. Then the girl imagines she is flying overhead. That is imaginary.	Make a list comparing something you could really do with your grandparent and something that could only happen through your imagination.	What would be fun to do with a relative if you could fly like Abuela does in this story? What would you want to see and where would you go?
Landmarks	Certain landmarks or even ordinary places are important to people because they remind them of special times in their lives.	Abuela and her granddaughter visit the Statue of Liberty because it represents a special time in Abuela's life: when she came to America.	Draw a picture of a "landmark" in your life. It could be a special building or some other place that is meaningful to you.	Why did you choose this particular landmark? Do you think your landmarks will change as you get older?
Family	Family members are very important, especially to little children.	Family is very important to the girl and her grandma as they take their imaginary trip They see Uncle Pablo, Aunt Elisa, and the girl's dad from high above the city.	Draw a picture and label the family members you would see if you were flying above your town.	How would these people look from far away? What would they be doing?
The Artist's Craft	The artist, Elisa Kleven, includes a lot of details in each of her collage illustrations.	Examine each page for colors, textures, and form.	Make a collage about how your house would look from way above.	How do you make a collage? Do you glue bits of fabric and newspaper and scraps together?

Book Hop

Apt. Three by Ezra Jack Keats.
Puffin, 1999. ISBN: 0670883425. Unpaginated.
Grades: PreK–2.

One rainy day two curious brothers discover who is playing the harmonica they hear in their apartment building. Notice Ezra Jack Keats' method of using collage and compare it to *Abuela*. Keats wrote and illustrated many books which are examples of how collage works to convey meaning and tone to a picture book. His works also depict characters of different ethnic backgrounds. Representative titles include: *Peter's Chair, Louie, The Snowy Day, Jennie's Hat, Pet Show!, Dreams, Hi, Cat!, My Dog is Lost!, A Letter to Amy, Goggles!, Whistle for Willie, Clementine's Cactus*, and others.

Classic Corner

The Empanadas that Abuela Made by Diane Gonzales Bertrand;
translated by Alex Pardo DeLange; illustrated by Gabriela Baeza Ventura.

Piñata, 2003. ISBN: 155885388X. Unpaginated.

Grades: PreK–2.

An add-along book that repeats all the ingredients needed for Grandmother to make empanadas (meat pies). The recipe is included.

For Older Children

Granny Torrelli Makes Soup by Sharon Creech; illustrated by Chris Raschka.

Joanna Cotler Books, Harper Trophy, 2003. ISBN: 0064409600. 141 pages.

Grades: 4–6.

Granny and 12-year-old Rosie bond as they get together in the kitchen to make cavatelli (pasta) and soup. This book spotlights the wisdom of the older generation and the positive influence of grandparents on their grandchildren's relationships.

Support Materials for *Abuela*

Awards and Honors
- Cooperative Children's Book Center, *50 Multicultural Books Every Child Should Read*: 2006
- National Council of Teachers of English, *Adventuring with Books: A Booklist for PreK–Grade 6*, 10th edition: 1993
- ALCS, American Library Association, *Children's Books on Aging*: 1993
- *Children's Catalog*, 18th edition: 2001
- ALSC, American Library Association, *Growing Up Latino in the U.S.A.*: 2004
- National Council of Teachers of English, *Kaleidoscope, a Multicultural Booklist for Grades K–8*: 1994

Reviews
- *Horn Book*: Spring 1991
- *Booklist*, Review Stars: October 15, 1991
- *Cooperative Children's Book Center Choices*: 1991
- *Kirkus*: August 15, 1991
- *The Five Owls*: November/December 1991

8.2

Tar Beach by Faith Ringgold.

Crown, 1991. ISBN: 0517580306. 32 pages.

Grades: K–2.

Synopsis

An eight-year-old African-American girl from Harlem in New York City experiences freedom when she dreams that she can fly through the sky. She calls her rooftop hideaway "tar beach" and imagines many wonderful possibilities from her view of the George Washington Bridge.

Booktalk

If you lived in a big city and you dreamed of feeling free, how would you pretend that you could get around? The girl in this book dreams that she is flying over the big city. She gets to see her father at work, her grandfather, and her mom. Let your imagination take you somewhere special. How would you describe it? Who would you take on your flight over the city?

Shelf-Esteem Connection

Your imagination can take you to places you never imagined.

THEME	MESSAGE	PLOT POINT CONNECTION	REINFORCING ACTIVITY	DISCUSSION QUESTIONS
Optimism	You can make things seem better in your mind.	The girl in the book calls her rooftop "tar beach."	Describe what you would bring up to your rooftop "tar beach" and why you would need it. Maybe you'll want to bring binoculars.	How does calling the rooftop "tar beach" help the girl feel better about herself and where she is living?
Connections	The girl, who narrates the story, feels a special connection to the George Washington Bridge.	She says the bridge is her most prized possession.	Make a list of your most prized possessions.	Why does the narrator feel a special connection to the GW Bridge? Is it because it opened on her birth day?
Using Similes	She says she wears the bridge like a diamond necklace.	Using the words *like* or *as*, she describes the bridge.	Using the words *like* or *as*, write down a description of your most prized possession.	How does the bridge look like a giant necklace? What does the bridge mean to the narrator of the story?
Dealing with Injustice	The girl wants to right the wrongs done to her grand-father because of prejudice.	The girl wants to "own" the building so that her grandfather will be accepted into the union.	Draw an example of prejudice that you have seen or experienced.	Why couldn't her grandfather join the union? How did that make the granddaughter feel?
Rewards Are Richly Deserved	The girl wants to have ice cream every night.	The narrator dreams she is flying over an ice cream factory.	Write down your favorite ice cream flavor and draw a picture of it.	What special treat would you would to share with your family?

Book Hop

Amazing Grace by Mary Hoffman; illustrated by Caroline Binch.
Dial, 1991. ISBN: 0803710402. Unpaginated.
Grades: PreK–2.

Although a classmate says that she cannot play Peter Pan in the school play because she is black, Grace discovers that she can do anything she sets her mind to do.

Classic Corner

I Speak English for My Mom by Muriel Stanek; illustrated by Judith Friedman.
Albert Whitman, 1989. ISBN: 0807536598. 32 pages.
Grades: K–2.

Lupe helps her mother Rosa Gomez learn English. The two moved to the United States from Mexico, and Lupe translates for her mother until her mom is able to enroll in an English class.

For Older Children

Ellington Was Not a Street by Ntozake Shange; illustrated by Kadir Nelson.
Simon & Schuster, 2004. ISBN: 0689828845. 40 pages.
Grades: All.

This poetic book pays tribute to African-American men such as Duke Ellington, Paul Robeson, Dizzy Gillespie, and W.E.B. DuBois. A Coretta Scott King Award winner (for illustrations).

Support Materials for *Tar Beach*

Awards and Honors
- Cooperative Children's Book Center, *50 Multicultural Books Every Child Should Read*: 2006
- American Library Association–Booklist Best First Novels for Youth: 1991
- Bank Street College of Education, Books to Read Aloud to Children of All Ages: 2003
- National Council of Teachers of English, *Kaleidoscope, A Multicultural Booklist for Grades K–8*: 1994
- *School Library Journal* Best Books: 1991
- Coretta Scott King Award: 1992
- Ezra Jack Keats New Writer Award: 1993
- *New York Times* Best Illustrated Children's Books of the Year: 1991
- Randolph Caldecott Medal Honor Book: 1992

Reviews
- *Horn Book*: May 1991
- *Kirkus*: January 15, 1990
- *Bulletin of the Center for Children's Books*: March 1991
- *The Five Owls*: March/April 1991

CHAPTER 9

Physical Challenges

9.1

Now One Foot, Now the Other by Tomie dePaola.
G.P. Putnam's Sons, 2005. ISBN: 0399242597. 48 pages.
Grades: PreK–3.

Synopsis
In this classic story originally published in 1981, Bobby's grandfather taught him to walk as a young boy. Roles reverse later in life when grandfather suffers the effects of a debilitating stroke, and Bobby helps him learn how to walk again.

Booktalk
Do you remember learning how to walk? Bobby's grandfather helped teach him how to walk. When Bobby grew older, his grandfather suffered a stroke. He didn't always know Bobby and struggled to talk and move his arms and legs. Bobby finds a special way to help his grandfather recover. Bobby manages to teach his grandpa something that his grandpa had taught *him* years before.

Shelf-Esteem Connection
Children can learn how to deal with the effects of a stroke, and they can help by sharing the things that they have learned.

THEME	MESSAGE	PLOT POINT CONNECTION	REINFORCING ACTIVITY	DISCUSSION QUESTIONS
Caring for Others	It is natural, and very important, to care about those around us and the problems that they have. This brings people closer together.	Bobby is very concerned when his grandpa is in the hospital. He hopes and wishes that his grandfather will get better soon.	Create get-well cards for Bobby's grandpa.	What are the fun things Bobby remembers doing with his grandfather? What does he look forward to doing with his grandfather again soon after his recovery?

(Cont'd.)

THEME	MESSAGE	PLOT POINT CONNECTION	REINFORCING ACTIVITY	DISCUSSION QUESTIONS
Remembering	When going through hard times, it is helpful to keep remembering the good times.	Bobby helps his grandfather remember by building the tower of blocks. Grandfather helped Bobby learn how to walk. Now Bobby is able to help him.	*Librarian:* Help the children create a bulletin board that shows pictures cut from magazines or family photographs illustrating how the generations help each other.	How do the youngsters and their families share family stories about the generations supporting each other in different ways through love and understanding?
Storytelling	Generations of families keep their stories alive through oral storytelling.	Grandfather Bob wants Bobby to tell him some stories while he recovers from the stroke.	Take turns in your group to "tell a story to Bob." Record the stories on an audiotape so it can be sent home.	What favorite activity would you do or what story would you tell to help Bobby's grandfather remember?
Taking Care of Yourself	It is very difficult to see a family member get sick and go to the hospital, but it is also crucial to take care of yourself. Not eating and not sleeping will not help the patient get better, and it could make you sick.	Bobby said that he didn't want to eat, and he had a hard time going to sleep at night while his grandfather was in the hospital.	Draw a picture to show how you would take care of yourself during a loved one's hospitalization.	What would you do to help the family out if you were Bobby?
Learning from Each Other	Young and old can learn from each other. People can reteach lessons to the persons who originally taught them.	Bobby helps his grandfather learn to walk in a way similar to the method Grandfather used to help him years ago.	Write a letter to Bobby's grandfather in your own words.	What can Bobby do when he misses his grandfather?

Book Hop

Faraway Grandpa by Roberta Karim; illustrated by Ted Rand.
Henry Holt, 2004. ISBN: 080506785X. 32 pages.
Grades: PreK–3.

Kathleen finds that her grandfather is becoming more and more forgetful. The book explains the facts about Alzheimer's disease and offers ways for families to cope with this illness.

Classic Corner

Singing with Mama Lou by Linda Jacobs Altman; illustrated by Larry Johnson.
Lee & Low, 2002. ISBN: 158430040X. Unpaginated.
Grades: PreK–3.

Momma Lou suffers from Alzheimer's disease, but that does not lessen the bond between granddaughter and grandmother. Tamika tries to help her grandmother regain her memory using photographs, school yearbooks, movie ticket stubs, and other memorabilia.

For Older Children

What's Happening to Grandpa? by Maria Shriver; illustrated by Sandra Speidel.
Little, Brown, 2004. ISBN: 0316001015. 48 pages.
Grades: 1–4.

Kate helps her grandfather, who is suffering from Alzheimer's, put together a scrapbook of old photographs designed to jog his memory and to help her come to terms with her grandfather's incapacity.

Support Materials for *Now One Foot, Now the Other*

Awards and Honors
- Virginia State Reading Association for Young Readers Program: 1989–90
- Cited in Harms, Jeanne McLain and Lucille Lettow, 1996. *Picture Books to Enhance the Curriculum*. New York: H.W. Wilson.
- *Best in Children's Books*: 1979–84
- *California Grandparents & Books Bibliography*: 1991–92
- *Best Books for Children: Preschool through Grade 6*. 7th edition. Bowker-Greenwood, 2002
- *Best Books for Children: Preschool through Grade 6*. 6th edition. R.R. Bowker, 1998
- *Best Books for Children: Preschool through Grade 6*. 5th edition. R.R. Bowker, 1994
- *Best Books for Children: Preschool through Grade 6*. 4th edition. R.R. Bowker, 1990
- Brodart Elementary School Library Collection: 1996

Reviews
- *Kirkus*: Fall 2005 (originally March 1, 1981)
- *Publishers Weekly*: 2005 (originally March 20, 1981)

9.2

Sara's Secret by Suzanne Wanous; illustrated by Shelly O. Haas.
Carolrhoda, 1995. ISBN: 0876148569. 40 pages.
Grades: 2–4.

Synopsis
Sara's younger brother, Justin, has cerebral palsy, and she struggles to come to terms with his condition. No one at school knows she has a brother, and she will not ride the same bus that her brother takes to school. She finally explains to her class about her brother's problems, and she finds that her friends have bigger hearts and more understanding than she originally anticipated.

Booktalk
Sara is ashamed that her brother, Justin, is physically challenged. Her mother doesn't understand why she doesn't want to ride the same bus that her brother takes to school. When Sara is

at school, she keeps her brother secret from the other children. One day, her teacher gives the class an assignment to bring one thing to school that would help someone with a disability. Sara leaves the room after one of her classmates shows his grandmother's hearing aide. Where is she going? What or who will she bring to the class?

Shelf-Esteem Connection

There is no need to keep disabilities a secret—one's own or that of a friend or a family member. People are far more accepting than one might think.

THEME	MESSAGE	PLOT POINT CONNECTION	REINFORCING ACTIVITY	DISCUSSION QUESTIONS
People Are Still People— Even with Their Disabilities	People with disabilities enjoy many of the same things that everyone else enjoys.	Justin likes the cookies mom bakes for him, especially because he can smell the warm, spicy scent as they are baking.	Make a list of the activities that Justin can participate in, such as listening to a book being read, tasking good food, and lying on his side to play with his toys.	What are the senses that Justin uses to enjoy the cookies?
Changing Attitudes	It is possible not only to accept but also to love those we once had an aversion to.	Sara explains to her class that Justin has cerebral palsy. He will not be able to read or write. But she can read to him.	Draw a picture or tell how Sara can help Justin.	Do you remember a time when you were ashamed of something and then changed your attitude?
Confidence	Confidence in the ability of others to be under-standing and compassionate will be rewarded.	Sara says she feels disap-pointed and embarrassed. She is not disappointed with the presentation. She is disappointed in herself. When she takes Justin back to his room after she brings him to her class, Sara admits that she was afraid to tell anyone about her brother. She thought they would not be friends with her anymore.	Write Sara a note telling her that you want to be her friend, and that she should not be afraid to tell her friends about Justin.	Can you remember a time when you began feeling more confident about something in your life?
Patience	One way to care for others is to be patient with them and take time to be with them.	Sara takes time to play with her brother and to make him more comfortable. Other times are really hectic, such as getting Justin ready for school, and it is not easy to be patient.	Write down the ways that you get ready for school on a busy morning. Tell how you can help make this routine go more smoothly.	What are some other ways you could help Justin?

(Cont'd.)

THEME	MESSAGE	PLOT POINT CONNECTION	REINFORCING ACTIVITY	DISCUSSION QUESTIONS
Sharing Skills	We should use our skills to help those who do not have those same skills.	Sara reads to her brother and tells him secrets. Sara tells her mom that she made puppets in art class so she can use them to play with Justin.	Make different puppets out of socks. Then role play with the puppets to dramatize the words and actions of the different characters in the book. This will help students empathize.	What are some games or activities that Sara might engage in with her younger brother Justin? What books could she read to him?

Book Hop

Nathan's Wish: A Story about Cerebral Palsy by Laurie Lears;
illustrated by Stacey Schuett.
Albert Whitman, 2005. ISBN: 0807571016. Unpaginated.
Grades: PreK–2.

At Miss Sandy's Raptor Rehabilitation Center, Nathan learns to care for a great horned owl that has a damaged wing. Through the comparison, Nathan learns that he can help others even though he is physically challenged.

Classic Corner

Susan Laughs by Jeanne Willis; illustrated by Tony Ross.
Henry Holt, 2000. ISBN: 0805065016. Unpaginated.
Grades: PreK–1.

Rhyming words show how a wheelchair-bound girl enjoys life. The focus is on her abilities.

For Older Children

Barry's Sister by Lois Metzger.
Atheneum, 1992. ISBN: 068931521X. 227 pages.
Grades: 4–7.

Ellen is a 12-year-old whose brother is afflicted with cerebral palsy. Ellen becomes obsessive about caring for Barry, but she eventually learns to strike a balance in her life.

Support Materials for *Sara's Secret*

Awards and Honors
• Recommended, *Horn Book*: Spring 1995
• *Baker & Taylor School Selection Guide K–8 Titles to Order*: 1998–99

Reviews
• *Booklist*: July 1, 1995
• *School Library Journal*: August 1, 1995

9.3

See You Tomorrow, Charles by Miriam Cohen; illustrated by Lillian Hoban.
Bantam Doubleday Dell, 1997. ISBN: 0440411513. 32 pages.
Grades: PreK–2.

Synopsis

Charles' disability, his blindness, has given him the opportunity to learn to "see" things with his hands. When his classmates get locked in a dark basement, he becomes a hero when they rely on him to feel the way out with his hands.

Booktalk

The students in Charles' class know that they shouldn't punch him. They know they need to take his hand to walk him out to the playground at recess. They know what to do and what not to do because Charles is blind. But what happens to Charles and the other students when they venture into a dark basement? How do they get out?

Shelf-Esteem Connection

People with disabilities often develop other skills that people who are not disabled do not master.

THEME	MESSAGE	PLOT POINT CONNECTION	REINFORCING ACTIVITY	DISCUSSION QUESTIONS
Respecting Others	Respect others regardless of their challenges. A disability can be turned into a capability.	Charles is learning to read with his fingers. This method of reading is called Braille.	*Librarian:* Distribute sample Braille cards to all students so that they can practice "reading" with their fingers instead of with their eyes. Point out that Braille can be found on signs in public restrooms and in elevators. Secure Braille alphabet cards through national organizations for the blind.	A soldier who became blind describes his mastery of Braille this way: "It's learning your ABC's again, just with bumps." What do you think he meant?
Role Models	Identifying with a positive role model can be empowering.	Charles' role model is Superman. He says he knows when Superman came to visit because of the way Superman smelled, and also that he was able to feel the letter "S" on his shirt.	Make alphabet letters by gluing sand, sandpaper, felt, or velvet fabric on top of alphabet forms. Feel the letters with your eyes closed.	Charles' hero is Superman. How does Charles become Superman to the class? Who is your hero? Why do you want to be like that hero?

(Cont'd.)

THEME	MESSAGE	PLOT POINT CONNECTION	REINFORCING ACTIVITY	DISCUSSION QUESTIONS
Tolerance	Promoting tolerance is important because it leads to developing respect.	Charles uses his hands to find a way out of the dark basement. The children allow him to lead the way, and Charles finds the door and the knob that gets them out.	Practice describing your use of all five senses when you are eating lunch or at snack time. How does the food smell? How does the food taste? What does it look like?	How did the children show their respect for Charles?
Focus on Strengths	Preconceptions can be changed by focusing on strengths instead of weaknesses.	The class is able to look beyond Charles' physical limitations and recognize his real strengths.	The teacher says: "It's lucky we have Charles in our class." Make a list of the different characters in the book and indicate their strengths—what they do best.	What do you feel are your special strengths? What do you like to do that you would want to do better?
Sensitivity	Being sensitive to others can help children build understanding of both their challenges and their strengths.	The children in the class learn to respect Charles' feelings. Anna Maria tells a classmate not to say "Look what I made" because Charles cannot see.	*Librarian:* Promote understanding and tolerance by having children act out various scenarios in the text.	What does Sammy mean when he says, "Sometimes he (Charles) might be sad because if he wanted to be a fireman and save somebody, he couldn't. He couldn't see the fire, or the people, or anything." How does Charles prove Sammy wrong?

Book Hop

A Picture Book of Helen Keller by David A. Adler;
illustrated by John and Alexandra Wallner.
Holiday House, 1990. ISBN: 0823408183. Unpaginated.
Grades: K–3.
This picture book tells the story of how Helen Keller dealt with being both blind and deaf.

Classic Corner

I Have a Sister—My Sister is Deaf by Jeanne Whitehouse Peterson;
illustrated by Deborah Ray.
Harper & Row, 1977 (reprinted 1984). ISBN: 0060247029. 32 pages.
Grades: K–3.
Peterson describes how her younger sister, who is deaf, experiences the world through the use of her other senses. Even though she cannot hear, her sister's sight, her sense of touch, her facial expressions, and her ability to use sign language are all keen. These methods allow her to communicate in a different, but no less effective, way.

For Older Children

Do You Remember the Color Blue? And Other Questions Kids Ask about Blindness
by Sally Hobart Alexander.
Viking, 2000. ISBN: 0670880434. 78 pages.
Grades: 5 and up.

Children ask questions of an author who lost her vision at the age of 27, including, "How did you become blind?" "How can you read?" and "Was it hard to be a parent when you couldn't see your kids?"

Support Materials for *See You Tomorrow, Charles*

Awards and Honors
- *Baker & Taylor School Selection Guide K–8 Titles to Order:* 1989
- *Best Books for Children*: *Preschool through the Middle Grades*. 3rd edition. R.R. Bowker, 1985
- *Best in Children's Books*: 1979–84

Reviews
- *Kirkus*: April 1, 1983

CHAPTER 10

Bullies

10.1

Bully by Judith Caseley.
Greenwillow, 2001. ISBN: 0688178677. Unpaginated.
Grades: PreK–3.

Synopsis
Judith Caseley based this story on her own father's youthful encounter with a bully. Following his father's good advice, with brave words and a good sense of humor, Mickey (the main character) learns how to turn Jack the Bully into Jack the Friend. Mickey's parents and his sister tell Mickey to use "brave" words and to try to be nice to Jack. But it turns out that Jack is acting out because he has a new sibling at home, and his is feeling neglected by his family.

Booktalk (Narrative)
Mickey says: "I have a problem with a boy at school named Jack. Jack eats my cookies at lunchtime and he breaks my pencils in half." It turns out that Jack's mother just had a new baby, and Jack isn't an only child anymore. Mickey says: "My dad says that most bullies are cowards. I wonder if that's true. I wonder if bringing Jack more cookies at lunchtime would help?"

Shelf-Esteem Connection
Respect, compassion, fairness, caring, and tolerance are the tools children can use to protect themselves against bullying behavior.

THEME	MESSAGE	PLOT POINT CONNECTION	REINFORCING ACTIVITY	DISCUSSION QUESTIONS
Compassion	Showing an interest in someone's family or showing some other kind of compassion will help someone to open up and drop bullying behavior.	When Mickey shows an interest in Jack's younger sister, Jack opens up and befriends him because he responds to compassion.	Draw a picture of some ways that Mickey can show Jack that he loves him as a friend.	Can you think of another way that Mickey can show Jack that he wants to be his friend?

(Cont'd.)

THEME	MESSAGE	PLOT POINT CONNECTION	REINFORCING ACTIVITY	DISCUSSION QUESTIONS
Feeling Good about Yourself	Feeling good about oneself can lead to better performance and good feelings about other people.	Jack feels good when he writes about how he made his new baby sister laugh for the first time. He writes about it, the teacher recognizes his effort with a star, and she gives him an excellent grade on his paper.	Write about how Jack feels about himself now that he has received a great grade on his paper.	What other ways can people help make Jack feel better?
Caring	Caring about a person is a good way to start a friendship.	There is a note on the blackboard that there is a class trip on Friday. Mickey prepares for the class trip by keeping Jack in mind.	Show in words and in a picture how Mickey prepares for Friday by keeping Jack in mind. Show in your drawing where you think the class is going on their trip.	Are you going to draw Mickey sitting next to Jack on the bus? Are you going to draw him bringing something special for lunch to share with Jack?
Understanding through Knowledge	Knowing what is causing someone to act like a bully is the first step toward understanding what to do.	Mama explains that Jack is not the only child anymore and reminds Mickey that when he was born, his sister wheeled him down the street and tried to give him away to a neighbor.	Mama suggests that Mickey be nice to Jack. Help Mickey think of ways to do that.	What can Mickey do for Jack to help him? What can Mickey do better with Jack as a friend?
Bravery	Often it is enough to act unafraid with a bully.	Papa tells Mickey to use brave words when speaking to Jack.	Make up a word wall of all of the brave words you can think of to help Mickey deal with Jack.	What are some "brave" words that you know?

Book Hop

Jungle Bullies by Steven Kroll; illustrated by Vincent Nguyen.
Marshall Cavendish, 2006. ISBN: 0761452973. Unpaginated.
Grades: PreK–1.

Monkey's mother offers a solution to the problem of bigger animals bullying smaller animals.

Classic Corner

Rotten Ralph by Jack Gantos; illustrated by Nicole Rubel.
Houghton Mifflin, 1976. ISBN: 0395242762. 48 pages.
Grades: PreK–2.

Ralph is Sarah's rotten cat, and he makes himself very difficult to bear. Finally, when the family takes Ralph to the circus, he learns about responsibility.

For Older Children

Jake Drake, Bully Buster by Andrew Clements; illustrated by Amanda Harvey.
Simon & Schuster, 2001. ISBN: 0689839170. 73 pages.
Grades: 2–4.

Link Baxter is a super bully who taunts and teases Jake, a fourth-grader. When they are asked to do a presentation for their class together, Jake finds out that Link is creative at model making, and sometimes Link even forgets to be mean when he is being creative. Jake also discovers that Link is afraid of public speaking, so Jake finds out that "behind every bully face, there's another face: a real face."

Support Materials for *Bully*

Awards and Honors
• Children's Book Council and the American Library Association, *Books and More for Growing Minds*: April 2001

Reviews
• *Booklist*: May 15, 2001
• *Bulletin of the Center for Children's Books*: June 2001
• *Horn Book*: Fall 2001
• *Kirkus*: March 1, 2001
• *Publishers Weekly* Children's Books: Spring 1996
• *School Library Journal*: June 1, 2001

10.2

Loudmouth George and the Sixth-Grade Bully by Nancy L. Carlson.
Carolrhoda, 2003 (20th anniversary edition). ISBN: 157505549X. Unpaginated.
Grades: PreK–3.

Synopsis
George is excited about going to school until Big Mike, an enormous sixth-grader, starts to bully him and steal his lunch. George and his friend Harriet come up with a plan to turn the tables on Big Mike and teach him a lesson.

Booktalk
Big Mike the Bully steals George's lunch repeatedly, and George tells his friend Harriet how afraid he is. What will George do to literally give Big Mike a taste of his own medicine? Harriet and George have an idea to outsmart Mike at his own game. They decide to add garlic to George's sandwich, vinegar to his soup, and hot pepper to his fruit dessert. To top it all off, they put lard (fat) on his cookies. This way they don't think Mike will want to steal George's lunch ever again. That is an extreme way to get back at Mike. What are some other ways Big Mike could learn to mend his ways?

Shelf-Esteem Connection

Humor can be a great buffer to use against bullying behavior.

THEME	MESSAGE	PLOT POINT CONNECTION	REINFORCING ACTIVITY	DISCUSSION QUESTIONS
Changing Your Perspective	Thinking about things from the other person's point of view helps a person's understanding of the situation.	George and Harriet have to outwit Mike the Bully at his own game. In order to do that, they need to see things from his point of view.	Use stick puppets to dramatize and role play the parts of George and Big Mike. Write down or dictate your feelings as you portray each character.	Have you ever been bothered by a bully? How did you handle the situation?
Humor	Humor is a big help in getting through difficult situations.	George and Harriet come up with an extreme—but humorous way—to get back at Mike.	Make up some come-back lines using humor to find a solution about how to react to bullying behavior.	What would you have done to deter a bully in the past?
Resolving Conflicts	There are ways to peacefully handle differences and disagreements.	Harriet and George add garlic to the sandwich, vinegar to the soup, and hot pepper to the dessert.	Write down an alternative solution to their problem without using food as the answer.	Who would you confide in if you had a problem with a bully? Would you tell a friend like Harriet?
Compromise	Sharing, taking turns, and compromising are excellent ways to deal with difficult attitudes of other people.	Harriet and George put lard on George's cookies so Mike won't steal them. There are other ways Harriet and George could have solved the problem. They could have shared the cookies, for example.	Draw a picture of another way Harriet and George could deal with Mike's behavior using the strategies of compromise, sharing, and taking turns.	Why do you think a bully acts the way he or she does?
Anthropomorphism: Animal Behavior Representing Human Behavior	Sometimes it is easier to solve problems when human qualities are shown as traits that animals display.	Harriet is a golden retriever and George is a rabbit, but they reflect and represent human feelings and emotions.	Make a list of the qualities that Harriet and George show that are human feelings and emotions.	Why is it sometimes easier to talk about problems such as bullying when animals act like people?

Book Hop

Bootsie Barker Bites by Barbara Bottner; illustrated by Peggy Rathmann.
G.P. Putnam's Sons, 1992. ISBN: 0399221255. Unpaginated.
Grades: PreK–2.
Bootsie Barker is a bully. The narrator has to find a creative way to put Bootsie, her tormentor, in her place.

Classic Corner

Brave Little Pete of Geranium Street by Rose and Samuel Lagercrantz;
illustrated by Eva Eriksson. Adapted by Jack Prelutsky.
Greenwillow, 1986. ISBN: 0688061788. 32 pages.
Grades: PreK–2.

In this classic Swedish tale, Pete eats a cake that makes him strong enough to face two bullies.

For Older Children

Mr. Lincoln's Way by Patricia Polacco.
Philomel, 2001. ISBN: 0399237542. Unpaginated.
Grades: 1–4.

Eugene Esterhause is a bully, and the principal of the school, Mr. Lincoln, finds a way to reach Mean Gene through his interest in birds.

Support Material for *Loudmouth George and the Sixth-Grade Bully*

Awards and Honors
• A Reading Rainbow Book

Reviews
• *Horn Book*: Fall 2003

10.3

Surviving Brick Johnson by Laurie Myers; illustrated by Dan Yaccarino.
Clarion, 2000. ISBN: 0395980313. 74 pages.
Grades: 2–4.

Synopsis

Alex decides to take karate lessons to defend himself against bully Brick Johnson. Then he finds out that Brick is not exactly what he appears to be. Brick has a softer side to him, and he even takes time to read to younger children. It turns out that Alex's assumptions about Brick are all wrong.

Booktalk (Narrative)

"I'm Alex and all along I thought Brick Johnson had it in for me. One day I imitated him at lunch, and he said, 'At my other school a boy did an imitation of me and . . . 'UH-OH!! I think he's going to maim me like Susan Green said. Maim is one of the vocabulary words for this week. My only chance is to take a karate class and try to bulk up. Mom says that maybe there is a peaceful solution. She says that sometimes bullies aren't as bad as they appear. Well, she doesn't know that Brick Johnson seems worse than how he appears! How am I going to defend myself against Brick—or make Brick Johnson my friend?"

Shelf-Esteem Connection

Sometimes people make incorrect assumptions about others. Getting to know them can lead to mutual respect and gaining a new friend.

THEME	MESSAGE	PLOT POINT CONNECTION	REINFORCING ACTIVITY	DISCUSSION QUESTIONS
Jumping to Conclusions	Jumping to conclusions can lead to harmful assumptions.	The karate master's room has a wise saying hanging on the wall: "Welcome the chance to learn about others." Alex had the wrong impression about Brick after all.	Pair children off and ask them to interview each other about their likes, their dislikes, and their pet peeves.	Can you think of a time when you "jumped to conclusions" about something and you were wrong?
Respecting Others	Respect for other people makes it possible to get to know them and avoid giving them inaccurate labels.	In their karate class, the students bow to show each other respect. Alex thinks that friends should bow to each other before playing Monopoly.	*Librarians:* Have books and Web sites available so that students can research a nonfiction book about Japan. Students will want to find out more about the Japanese custom of bowing (instead of our American custom of shaking hands). Ask the older group to write down some facts about Japanese culture and customs.	How did Alex build things up in his mind concerning what Brick would do to him?
Heroes	Heroes are people to look up to and emulate.	Alex keeps some baseball cards with him at all times. He says that makes him feel more confident because baseball heroes inspire him.	Make up a few hero cards starring people who inspire you. Then read a biography about one of those people. If one isn't written yet, you can write about someone you know who personally inspires you.	Who are your heroes in the movies? Who are your heroes in comic books? Who are your heroes in real life?
Persistence	Persistence leads to improvement.	Alex's karate teacher, Walt, tells his student to "Keep trying," and "You'll get it." Walt tells Alex he is a "work in progress," a phrase Alex likes because it makes him feel that he doesn't *have* to be perfect.	Write about or draw a picture showing something you could not do at first, but eventually learned how to do.	Can you think of a time when you had to learn to do something, and it took many tries, but then you finally got it?
Different Aspects of People	People have different sides to them, depending upon who is looking. Getting to know someone may unveil surprising aspects.	Alex finds out that Brick reads books to the younger students at school.	A student could also be a son and a grandson and a nephew and a citizen. Draw a picture of the different roles one person can play. Show how people can bring different parts of their personalities to the different roles they play.	What different roles do you play? For example, you could be a son, a daughter, a niece, an aunt, a grandson, a student, and so on.

Book Hop

Myrtle by Tracey Campbell Pearson.
Farrar, Straus & Giroux, 2004. ISBN: 0374351570. Unpaginated.
Grades: PreK–2.

Myrtle and her brother take Aunt Tizzy's advice about how to face Frances, the mean, bullying neighbor next door. African masks give them the courage to put Frances in her place.

Classic Corner

Happy Birthday to You, You Belong in the Zoo by Diane deGroat.
Morrow, 1999. ISBN: 0688165451. 32 pages.
Grades: PreK–2.

Gilbert is invited to Lewis' birthday party. He wants to buy him a frying pan as a present because Lewis is bossy. Mom switches the gift at the last minute and saves Gilbert from embarrassment. Lewis has a change of heart in the process.

For Older Children

Good Grief . . . Third Grade by Colleen O'Shaughnessy McKenna.
Scholastic, 1993. ISBN: 0590451235. 151 pages.
Grades: 3–5.

Marsha Cessano wants to start third grade on the right foot, but she is paired off in class with Roger Friday, who seems to be a real bully. Marsha tells a lie that ends up with a suspension from school for Roger.

Support Material for *Surviving Brick Johnson*

Awards and Honors
• Bank Street College of Education, *Best Children's Books of the Year*: 2001
• American Library Association–American Library Association for Services to Children, Notable Books for Children: 2001
• Parent's Guide to Children's Media: 2001
• Black-Eyed Susan Book Award Nominee: 2002–03
• Great Stone Face Award Nominee, New Hampshire: 2001–02

Reviews
• *Booklist*: September 15, 2000
• *Bulletin of the Center for Children's Books*: November 2000

CHAPTER **11**

Alcoholism

11.1

Banana Beer by Carol Carrick; illustrated by Margot Apple.
Albert Whitman, 1995. ISBN: 0807505684. Unpaginated.
Grades: K–3.

Synopsis
Charlie is a young orangutan who has difficulty coping with his father's drinking problem. His teacher, Miss Lovewell, offers him encouragement. She tells him that his dad always loves him, and that his dad isn't angry with him. She explains that he becomes angry because he has tried to stop drinking and has not been able to succeed. Charlie hopes that his dad will get help for himself someday soon.

Booktalk
Alcoholism is a disease, and people who have it drink way too much. Family members often suffer as much as the loved one who drinks. Sometimes it is very hard to understand this disease. We need to learn that the other person's drinking is not our fault. We did not cause the disease, we cannot control it, and we cannot cure it. Charlie the orangutan in our story deals with his dad's drinking problem by not relying on his father's behavior when he drinks or on his promises to stop. Charlie learns to rely on himself.

Shelf-Esteem Connection
An alcoholic's problem is not anyone else's fault. Family members can only love the alcoholic, take care of themselves, and cope by finding someone to talk to.

THEME	MESSAGE	PLOT POINT CONNECTION	REINFORCING ACTIVITY	DISCUSSION QUESTIONS
Taking Care of Yourself	When people do something special for themselves or give themselves the things they	Miss Lovewell tells Charlie to learn to be happier by doing one of his	Make a list of things you like to do that Charlie might enjoy doing, too. Then draw a picture of the	What good things do you do for yourself each day?

(Cont'd.)

THEME	MESSAGE	PLOT POINT CONNECTION	REINFORCING ACTIVITY	DISCUSSION QUESTIONS
Taking Care of Yourself *(Cont'd.)*	need, they are not being selfish. They are taking care of themselves.	favorite things every day.	two of you enjoying this activity together.	
Communication	Communicating your problems with someone older whom you can trust can help you feel better.	Charlie finds out that it is OK to talk to Miss Lovewell about Daddy's drinking. Before, he says, he wasn't able to talk to anyone about it.	Decide which means of communication works best for you. Would you rather talk to someone directly, write a letter, write an e-mail, or draw a picture to express your feelings of concern?	Whom do you feel you could talk to about almost anything?
Keeping Yourself Safe	People need to have a safe place to go if they need help.	Miss Lovewell tells Charlie that he has a grown-up friend in her and that she cares about him. Charlie says he felt happy and safe at school.	Make sure there is someone you know whom you can talk to about a problem or question you may have. Make up a list of addresses and phone numbers of places where you feel safe.	Do you have a safe place to go to if needed? Where is that place?
Handling Emergencies	It is important to know what problems you could tell about to other people and which people would be appropriate to tell.	Charlie was afraid to talk to anyone about dad's drinking problem.	Make a list of people you could talk to in case of an emergency.	Who would you contact in an emergency?
Empathy	Try to understand when someone you know has a problem.	Charlie says that he hopes his dad takes him to the beach when he feels better. But if he's sick again, he'll try not to mind. He is learning to be tolerant and understanding of someone else who has a serious problem.	Draw a picture of Charlie and his dad having fun times at the beach together.	How do you, by being understanding, help someone else who has a problem?

Book Hop

My Dad by Niki Daly.
Simon & Schuster/M.K. McElderry, 1995. ISBN: 0689506201. Unpaginated.
Grades: K–3.

A brother and sister are embarrassed by their father's alcoholism. Alcoholics Anonymous helps him recognize that he has an illness, and the people in the group teach Dad to focus on what is important in his life.

Classic Corner

I Wish Daddy Didn't Drink So Much by Judith Vigna.
Albert Whitman, 1988. ISBN: 0807535230. 40 pages.
Grades: K–3.

Lisa's mother and her neighbor offer advice when Lisa struggles to live with her father's drinking problem. They both help Lisa with positive ways to handle her problem-filled home situation.

For Older Children

The Road to Paris by Niki Grimes.
G. P. Putnam's Sons, 2006. ISBN: 0399245375. 153 pages.
Grades: 4–8.

In this Coretta Scott King Honor Book, an eight-year-old girl named Paris Richmond had been placed in a foster family while her mother received treatment. She now has to decide about whether or not to rejoin her rehabilitated alcoholic mother.

Support Materials for *Banana Beer*

Awards and Honors
• Recommended, *Horn Book Guide*: Fall 1995

Reviews
• *Horn Book Guide*: Fall 1995
• *Bulletin of the Center for Children's Books*: April 1995

11.2

Bottles Break by Nancy Maria Grande Tabor.
Charlesbridge, 1999. ISBN: 0881063177. Unpaginated.
Grades: K–3.

Synopsis

A child describes how he feels when his mother drinks. He finds bottles all over the house. Although bottles seem beautiful when they come in different shapes and sizes, in this case, they cause pain and suffering. The child explains how drinking makes people feel empty inside and somehow causes people to act very strangely. The child confides in his teacher, and his teacher explains that alcoholism is not the child's fault. She suggests that the child ride a bike, read a book, play with friends, or write in a journal. The book ends on a hopeful note that the parent will receive help.

Booktalk

Bottles can be beautiful because they can be different shapes and sizes. They can also be hurtful when they are empty bottles, broken and tossed about. When people have a disease like alcoholism, they drink and keep on drinking because it becomes a habit. The child in this book does not want his mom to drink any more. He tells his teacher and writes down his feelings.

He knows that his mother's drinking is not his fault. And his teacher gives him ideas of what to do when he is feeling bad about his mother and his drinking. He can ride his bike, read a book, write in his journal, or play with his friends.

Shelf-Esteem Connection
It is possible to handle rough times by confiding in a responsible adult and by doing things to feel better.

THEME	MESSAGE	PLOT POINT CONNECTION	REINFORCING ACTIVITY	DISCUSSION QUESTIONS
Self-respect	People need to respect themselves and learn ways to do what is best for themselves.	The narrator is not proud of his mother. But he can learn to understand what to do to help himself in a difficult situation.	Make a list (or dictate a list) of what you can do for yourself when you feel down or sad.	How can difficulties sometimes be turned around? How does the narrator have a chance to become closer to his teacher?
Empathy	Seeing things from another person's point of view leads to sympathy and understanding.	Even though the narrator cannot understand his mother's drinking problem, he knows that he still wants to play with her and talk with her.	Draw a picture showing you and your mom doing something special together.	The narrator says he feels bigger and bigger every day. How can you feel bigger and more grown up each day?
Helping Others and Helping Ourselves	By learning about how other people cope with various challenges, people can learn to help others and to help themselves in the process.	The narrator tries to do things that make him feel better.	Describe what you can do to make yourself and your feelings "count."	The narrator says he sometimes feels very small at the beginning of the book. Then at the end, he says he is getting bigger. Is he really growing physically bigger? Or is he getting stronger and more self-confident?
Communication	There are many ways to communicate: words, hands, bodies, and gestures are all ways to express oneself.	The boy is shown as a drawing that bends.	Draw a picture to show how you feel when you feel good about yourself.	What colors would you choose to use in your picture Would you draw a small picture of yourself or a larger one? Why?
Awareness	The more we learn about others and different ways of coping, the more respect we instill.	The narrator talks about how bottles can be beautiful . . . or they can be destructive.	Write or dictate a paragraph about something you can think of that can be used for good or for not so good, just like the bottles in this book.	Would you think about someone differently if you were aware that the person had a problem and needed help?

Book Hop

An Elephant in the Living Room by Marian H. Typpo and Jill M. Hastings.
Hazelden Activity Book, 1994. ISBN: 1568380348. 129 pages.
Grades: 3–5.

This illustrated book will help children and their families understand and learn to cope with the problem of alcoholism in their family.

Classic Corner

Sometimes My Mom Drinks Too Much by Kevin Kenny and Helen Krull;
illustrated by Helen Cogancherry.
Raintree, 1980. ISBN: 081721366X. 31 pages.
Grades: 1–3.

Maureen tries to cope with her mother's illness; her feelings are very conflicted about her mom's dependence on alcohol.

For Older Children

Evangeline Brown and the Cadillac Motel by Michele Ivy Davis.
Dutton, 2004. ISBN: 0525472215. 181 pages.
Grades: 4–6.

After Evangeline Dawn Brown's mother passes away, her father becomes an alcoholic. They both live at the Cadillac Motel in Paradise, Florida. Eddie's (Evangeline's nickname) hopes rise when her teacher shows an interest in her.

Support Material for *Bottles Break*

Reviews
• *School Library Journal*: Spring 1999

11.3

No Way, Slippery Slick! by Joanne Oppenheim, Barbara Brenner, William Hooks, and Bank Street College of Education; illustrated by Joan Auclair.
HarperCollins, 1991. ISBN: 0061074381. 32 pages.
Grades: K–2.

Synopsis

Slippery Slick, a tricky cat, tries to lure Clever Kitten into dangerous situations. Each and every time Clever finds that his resolve is tested, and each and every time he defends himself and his health. By telling Slippery that he always needs his mom's permission, he never takes medicine by himself, and he does not deliver secret packages, he becomes more self-reliant.

Booktalk

Has anyone ever asked you to do something that you knew deep down inside of you was wrong? How did you respond? Did you walk away? Did you have just the right answer to defend yourself? In this book, a tricky cat named Slippery Slick tries to get Clever Kitten to get into risky situations. Will Clever always have the right answer to put Slippery in his place?

Shelf-Esteem Connection
It is a good idea to be prepared and to have responses ready for when safety is at stake.

THEME	MESSAGE	PLOT POINT CONNECTION	REINFORCING ACTIVITY	DISCUSSION QUESTIONS
Doing What Is Right	It is not necessary to listen to someone who asks people to do something wrong or dangerous.	The narrator is proud. The narrator respects himself and his healthy way of living.	Role-play the parts of Clever and Slippery. Reinforce Clever's responses each time he defends himself against dangerous or illegal behaviors.	How can difficulties turn into positives? How does Clever defend himself and his positive choices?
Protecting Yourself	It is crucial for people to protect their own health and well-being.	Clever does not want to go off with someone he doesn't know. He doesn't want to take medicine offered to him from someone other than his parent. He doesn't want to "deliver secret packages."	Clever the Cat knows answers to defend himself, such as, "I never take medicine by myself," and "I don't deliver secret packages." Draw a picture of you helping Clever deliver his positive messages to Slippery Slick.	You need to build your own defense vocabulary. What words could you use to defend yourself against Slippery?
Help Others and Helping Ourselves	By learning about how other people cope with various challenges, one can learn to help them and also to help oneself in the process.	The narrator can try to help others to defend themselves by teaching them the right vocabulary.	Partner in the room and volley words back and forth to try to defend positive behavior.	How did you feel when you were able to out-talk Slippery?
Communication	Body language can be used to express or to defend oneself.	The narrator turns his back on Slippery, tries to distance himself from Slippery, and defends his pride by always saying: "No Way, Slippery Slick, No Way."	Draw some pictures to show how you would get away from Slippery Slick and what your saying (or mantra) would be, such as "Go away, No way, I won't do it!"	What are the different ways you could use to get your message across to Slippery Slick so that he won't bother you again?
Believing in Yourself	It is necessary for people to believe in themselves if they want to defend themselves.	The narrator feels good about himself, so he doesn't need to listen to Slippery's negative words.	Write a paragraph or two about how good you feel about yourself.	What are some positive things you can do to help yourself feel empowered? Can you learn karate, for example? You can take out a book about karate from your library.

Book Hop

Daddy Doesn't Have to Be a Giant Anymore by Jane Resh Thomas;
illustrated by Marcia Sewall.
Clarion, 1996. ISBN: 0395694272. 46 pages.
Grades: PreK–2.

Dad becomes a giant when he sneaks into the garage and starts drinking alcohol. Family members convince Dad to enter a treatment program.

Classic Corner

Danger: Drugs and Your Parents by E. Rafaela Picard.
Powerkids, 1997. ISBN: 0823950506. 24 pages.
Grades: 2–5.

This book from The Drug Awareness Library informs children about adults' possible chemical dependency and how to go about getting help.

For Older Children

When Someone in the Family Drinks Too Much by Richard C. Langsen;
illustrated by Nicole Rubel.
Dial, 1996. ISBN: 0803716869. Unpaginated.
Grades: 1–4.

This book is a "self-help guide" to help children cope with alcoholism in the family setting. It features a cast of bears that allows children a safe distance while the text delivers the moral of the story. Thus, the material is presented gently through the safety of drawn characters.

Support Material for *No Way Slippery Slick!*

Awards and Honors
• *A Child's First Book about Drugs*, created by Bank Street College of Education

Reviews
• *Project Healthy Choices*, a substance-abuse program developed by Bank Street College, 1991

CHAPTER 12

Illness and Death

12.1

Blow Me a Kiss, Miss Lilly by Nancy White Carlstrom;
illustrated by Amy Schwartz.
Harper & Row, 1990. ISBN: 0060210138. 32 pages.
Grades: PreK–2.

Synopsis

Sara is best friends with Miss Lilly, the elderly woman who lives across the street. Miss Lilly's cat, Snug, is the third part of this triad. Sara has special moments with Miss Lilly until Miss Lilly's illness and death. Sara finds comfort with the cat Snug and by tending Miss Lilly's garden.

Booktalk

Friends can be your age, but they can also be much older or younger than you are. Sara has a special friendship with her neighbor, Miss Lilly, who is much older than she is. They share many happy events: stories, picnics, and chores in the garden. They also share something sad when Miss Lilly gets sicks and dies. Even with the sadness, do you think Sara is sorry she befriended her elderly friend?

Shelf-Esteem Connection

Grandparents are not the only elderly adults with whom children can share close relationships. People from different generations can learn from each other.

THEME	MESSAGE	PLOT POINT CONNECTION	REINFORCING ACTIVITY	DISCUSSION QUESTIONS
Storytelling	Stories from the past tell us a lot about our present and our future.	Miss Lilly told Sara stories about when she was a girl.	"Interview" someone in your neighborhood or in your family about when they were younger. Try to obtain a photograph and a few quotes to share with others.	What words of advice can you recall from someone older than you?

(Cont'd.)

THEME	MESSAGE	PLOT POINT CONNECTION	REINFORCING ACTIVITY	DISCUSSION QUESTIONS
Making Decisions	Once people grow up they are able to make decisions for themselves instead of always asking someone older.	Miss Lilly can eat ice cream for breakfast and ice cream for lunch. She says she can do that at her age. She has earned the right to do it.	Draw a picture of what you would like to eat or what you would like to do at breakfast time and at lunch time that you wouldn't ordinarily do.	What would you do first on a "backwards kind of day?"
Kindness to Others	When people are kind to others, everyone feels good.	Miss Lilly knew everyone's birthday and she would make them a floral bouquet and a card. She even gave the grumpy man down the street flowers and a card. After she did that, Sara wasn't afraid of him anymore.	Make a birthday card and draw a flowery picture for someone you know who will be celebrating a birthday soon.	Can you recall how good it made you feel when you did something nice for someone else?
Planning for the Future	It is important to think about the future and to be prepared.	Sara and Miss Lilly picked the plums from her tree and boiled them to put them in jars to make plum jelly.	List other events that Sara might have to prepare for when she has an elderly friend.	If you could save something to use in the future, what would it be?
Accepting Responsibility	Accepting responsibility gives you something to do for someone else and makes you feel better.	When Miss Lilly dies, Sara takes on the responsibility of caring for Snug, the cat, and she also helps tend to Miss Lilly's garden.	Draw a picture of Sara and Snug the cat in Miss Lilly's garden.	What are some responsibilities you have toward neighbors?

Book Hop

Loop the Loop by Barbara Dugan; illustrated by James Stevenson.
Greenwillow, 1992. ISBN: 0688096476. Unpaginated.
Grades: PreK–3.

This is book about an intergenerational friendship between a girl and a senior citizen. The relationship continues even after the woman enters a nursing home.

Classic Corner

Miss Rumphius by Barbara Cooney.
Viking, 1982. ISBN: 0670479586. 32 pages.
Grades: PreK–3.

Great-Aunt Alice Rumphius promises that when she grows up she will travel, live near the sea in her old age, and do something to make the world more beautiful.

For Older Children

Miss Tizzy by Libba Moore Gray; illustrated by Jada Rowland.
Simon & Schuster, 1993. ISBN: 0671775901. Unpaginated.
Grades: K–4.

Miss Tizzy always took care of and entertained the children in her neighborhood. When she becomes ill, it is their turn to supply her with songs, laughs, and presents.

Support Material for *Blow Me a Kiss, Miss Lilly*

Awards and Honors
• *Baker & Taylor School Selection Guide K–8 Titles to Order*: 1991–95
• *Best Books for Children: Preschool through Grade 6*. 5th edition. R. R. Bowker, 1994
• *Best Books for Children: Preschool through Grade 6*. 6th edition. R. R. Bowker, 1998
• *Best Books for Children: Preschool through Grade 6*. 7th edition. Bowker-Greenwood, 2001
• *Children's Catalog*. 16th edition. H. W. Wilson, 1991

Reviews
• *Booklist* Monthly Selections: 1988–1990
• *Horn Book*: July 1990
• *School Library Journal*: July 1990

12.2

Good Luck, Mrs. K! by Louise Borden; illustrated by Adam Gustavson.
Simon & Schuster/M. K. McElderry, 1999. ISBN: 0689821476. Unpaginated.
Grades: 2–5.

Synopsis
A beloved third-grade teacher becomes hospitalized with cancer. The students send her notes and drawings and promise to keep reading while they are taught by a substitute and wait for her return to the classroom.

Booktalk (Narrative)
"We all think that Mrs. Kempchinski is the best third-grade teacher around. She remembers all our names. She takes us everywhere in the world through books. She called us her 'third-grade detectives and her third-grade travelers.' Her favorite mottos are: 'Be good listeners' and 'Remember to read.' When we studied worms, we read lots of books about worms. Then we looked at worms close up. Then we wrote about worms. We even wore plastic worm earrings and ate candy worms for snack time. Mrs. K even does a homework dance when we hand in our work on time. She makes school so much fun! That's why we were so upset when we found out that Mrs. K was sick. We made her cards and get-well notes. The whole class was invited back to school the day after school let out for the summer. The principal wanted us to welcome back a very special guest. 'And that guest was . . . ?'"

Shelf-Esteem Connection

It is especially difficult for students when a favorite teacher is ill, but it helps to remember her with cards and letters.

THEME	MESSAGE	PLOT POINT CONNECTION	REINFORCING ACTIVITY	DISCUSSION QUESTIONS
Being Thoughtful	Receiving cards and notes tells someone who is hospitalized or sick that people are thinking of him or her.	Mrs. K's class wrote notes and made cards for her when she was in the hospital to let her know they were thinking of her.	Write a note and draw a get-well card for someone you know is sick or in the hospital.	What are some thoughtful things you can do for someone who is ill?
Unanswerable Questions	Adults don't always know the answers.	The children ask the principal, Mr. Rivers, "How many operations does it take to cure cancer?" His reply was that there are some answers even principals don't know.	Mrs. K does come back to school in the fall. Write a letter to welcome Mrs. K back to school.	Did you know that sometimes you have to look in more than one place to find answers to difficult questions? Where would you look?
Adjusting to Change	It is difficult to adjust to a new person, particularly when a well-loved person is being replaced.	Mrs. K did special dances when the students handed in their homework on time. They wanted Mrs. K back—Mrs. Dodd, their substitute teacher, did not know any homework dances. Still, they had to adjust to Mrs. Dodd.	Make up a special dance for your own class. Then write down the instructions so a substitute librarian can understand the dance.	What can you do to be helpful to a new substitute teacher or librarian?
Learning from Each Other	Everyone can learn something from others, parents from children and teachers from students.	Even though Mrs. K was their teacher, she said she wanted to learn *from* her students.	Choose a special book to read to a favorite person. Select something you know that person will enjoy.	What book would you want the substitute teacher or librarian to read to the class?
Teachers and Librarians Are Special People	A good teacher or librarian is a special gift.	The third-graders loved their teacher because she made learning fun.	Write down some of the tricks the students could teach Mrs. Dodd. For example, they could teach her some of the homework dances they learned from Mrs. K.	What can you teach your teacher or librarian how to do?

Book Hop

I Remember Miss Perry by Pat Brisson; illustrated by Stéphane Jorisch. Dial, 2006. ISBN: 9780803729810. Unpaginated. Grades: K–3.

The students' teacher is involved in a fatal car accident. The students' memories of Miss Perry help them get through a very, very difficult time.

Classic Corner

Miss Nelson Is Missing by Harry Allard and James Marshall.
Houghton Mifflin, 1977. ISBN: 0395252962. 32 pages.
Grades: PreK–2.

The kids in Room 207 take advantage of their teacher's good nature until she disappears and they are faced with a vile substitute.

For Older Children

Remembering Mrs. Rossi by Amy Hest; illustrated by Heather Malone.
Candlewick, 2007. ISBN: 9780763621636. 192 pages.
Grades: 3–5.

Eight-year-old Annie Rossi, a third grader in New York City, misses her mom who recently passed away. Her mom's former pupils create a book called "Remembering Mrs. Rossi," which comforts both Annie and her father at such a difficult time.

Support Material for *Good Luck, Mrs. K!*

Awards and Honors
• Christopher Awards Winner: 2000
• Bank Street College of Education, *Best Children's Books of the Year*: 1999
• *Best Books for Children*, 7th edition: 2002
• Ohio Buckeye Children's Book Awards, All Grades: 1999
• South Carolina Children's Book Award Nominee: 1997–98
• Texas Bluebonnet Award: 1998–2003

Reviews
• *Booklist*: July 1, 1999
• *Bulletin of the Center for Children's Books*: July 1999
• *Kirkus*: May 1, 1999
• *Publishers Weekly*: May 17, 1999
• *School Library Journal*: May 1, 1999
• *New York Times Book Review*: October 17, 1999

12.3

Nana Upstairs and Nana Downstairs by Tomie dePaola.
G. P. Putnam's Sons, 1998. ISBN: 0399231080. 32 pages.
Grades: PreK–3.

Booktalk

How can Nana be upstairs and downstairs at the same time? Tommy is lucky because he has a grandmother and a great-grandmother, and he loves them both very much. Nana Upstairs is very old, 94 candles on her cake, in fact. She likes sharing candy with Tommy. Tommy watched when Nana Downstairs combed Nana Upstairs' long, silver hair. Even though Tommy's brother said Nana Upstairs looked like a witch, Tommy thought she was beautiful. They took lots of pictures together, with Tommy standing between his grandmothers. Then Tommy found that Nana Upstairs' bed was empty and his mother explained that she had died. She told him Nana will always live on in his memories. On night he sees a falling star and his mother tells him it might be a kiss from Nana Upstairs. Many years later, when Nana Downstairs is quite old, she dies, too. Tommy sees another star fall from the sky. Now he calls both grandmothers Nana Upstairs. What other ways can he remember them?

Shelf-Esteem Connection
Even though loved ones die, their treasured memories stay alive.

THEME	MESSAGE	PLOT POINT CONNECTION	REINFORCING ACTIVITY	DISCUSSION QUESTIONS
Keeping Memories Alive	Whenever people think and talk about a loved one, they are keeping the loved one's memories alive.	Tommy can recall memories of Nana Upstairs and Nana Downstairs whenever he thinks about them. Nana Downstairs loved to cook, and Tommy remembers standing by the big black stove in the kitchen. Nana Upstairs liked to eat candy. Both grandmothers liked to have their hair combed.	Make a journal of special activities you do with your grandparents. Think of what they like to do on their own and activities that you enjoy doing together.	What are some of the favorite activities you do with your grandparents?
Following through with Actions	There are many ways to keep memories alive.	Tommy names a falling star for each of his nanas.	Draw a picture of a falling star and name it for someone special, just as Tommy did.	What are some unique ways you can remember a special person?
Family Pride	Parents and their parents are people of whom to be proud. That is why it is important to save the memories of them and their stories.	Tommy spends a lot of time with his grandmother and great-grandmother, so he knows about previous generations of his family.	*Librarian:* Ask children to bring in photographs and talk about family members. Determine the different countries from which these relatives came to America.	Discuss about whether these relatives were immigrants or if they were born in this country.
Remembering with Your Five Senses	All five senses can help people remember the special people in their lives.	Tommy used his senses to remember Nana Upstairs and Nana Downstairs. For example, he remembered the taste of the candy mints and of cake. He remembered what they looked like and what their hair felt like.	You can remember a person using more than just your sense of sight. Think about how you can use all of your senses and write about how someone you loved looked, felt, sounded, and so on.	How can you describe your grandparents (or other relatives) using your five senses?

(Cont'd.)

THEME	MESSAGE	PLOT POINT CONNECTION	REINFORCING ACTIVITY	DISCUSSION QUESTIONS
Pictures, Photos, and Memories	Memory is like a camera. It is possible to store pictures with the mind to remember at some future time.	Mother tells Tommy that "She (Nana) will come back in your memory whenever you think about her."	Draw a picture of a special person you wish to remember.	Share special photographs of your grandparents and write a short story about one the photos. Talk about what you (or other people) are doing in the photo.

Book Hop

A Handful of Seeds by Monica Hughes; illustrated by Luis Garay.
Orchard, 1996. ISBN: 0531094987. Unpaginated.
Grades: K–3.

Concepcion's grandmother's legacy is to tell her granddaughter to always have seeds for planting so that she will have enough to eat. Concepcion honors her grandmother by planting seeds to grow beans, chili peppers, and corn. She resurrects her garden by replanting after it is trampled upon.

Classic Corner

The Hundred Penny Box by Sharon Bell Mathis; illustrated by Leo and Diane Dillon.
Viking, 1975. ISBN: 0670387878. 47 pages.
Grades: 1–4.

Michael has a special relationship with his 100-year-old Great-Great-Aunt Dew. She keeps a penny for every year of her life. Michael's mother doesn't understand the significance of the box and wants to throw it away. Aunt Dew says, "Them's my years in that box. That's me in that box."

For Older Children

Family Pride
Make up a family tree to show to the children and to introduce the concept of genealogy. Identify the students who are lucky enough to have grandparents and great-grandparents who are still living. Help them make their draw their own family trees.

Support Material for *Nana Upstairs and Nana Downstairs*

Awards and Honors
• *Best Books, Children's Catalog*, 18th edition: 2001

Reviews
• *Booklist*: February 15, 1998
• *Horn Book*: Fall 1998
• *Kirkus*: July 1, 1973
• *Publishers Weekly*: April 24, 2000

12.4

Remember the Butterflies by Anna Grossnickle Hines.
Dutton, 1991. ISBN: 0525446796. 32 pages.
Grades: K–4.

Synopsis

When Grandpa dies, Holly and Glen remember the special times they had together, garden-ing, reading, and learning about butterflies. Anna Hines' book about the difficulty of coming to terms with a loved one's death is an outgrowth of the troubling emotions her own children experienced when their grandfather died. By focusing on the life cycle of a butterfly, Hines captures the essence of honoring a life well lived.

Booktalk

Holly and Glen are lucky because their grandfather has a beautiful garden where the flowers attract lots of butterflies. One day they find a butterfly in the garden that is not moving. Grandpa explains that he cannot fix a creature that is no longer alive. He says to look for the eggs because the butterfly must have laid eggs before it died. The eggs will hatch into caterpillars, and the caterpillars will change into more butterflies. "Let's celebrate the butterfly's life," Grandpa says. One day Grandpa dies, and everyone remembers what they loved about him. Glen and Holly's mom help them to remember that Grandpa will live on through his family members. What do they remember most? What do they want to do to celebrate Grandpa's life?

Shelf-Esteem Connection

Memories and actions will help people live on even after they have died.

THEME	MESSAGE	PLOT POINT CONNECTION	REINFORCING ACTIVITY	DISCUSSION QUESTIONS
Honoring Memories	There are many different ways to show our feelings for a loved one.	Grandpa and Holly and Glen watched the changes from caterpillar to chrysalis and finally, to butterfly. The dying butterfly leaves behind its eggs to hatch, just as grandparents leave behind memories for their children and grandchildren to share.	Make a journal of special times Glen and Holly shared with their grandfather, what they noticed, and what they watched out for in the garden.	How can you show your feelings to a beloved person?
The Life Cycle	The butterfly lived on because of the eggs that it left behind.	Holly and Glen enjoyed working with Grandpa in the garden, sitting on his lap, feeling his scratchy beard, listening to him read stories, and watching him wink at them. They especially enjoyed all that they learned about butterflies.	Make a book about butterflies and dedicate it to someone special whom you want to remember.	What were some of the important lessons that Grandfather taught Holly and Glen about the life cycle?

(Cont'd.)

THEME	MESSAGE	PLOT POINT CONNECTION	REINFORCING ACTIVITY	DISCUSSION QUESTIONS
Remembering through Actions	Doing something constructive is helpful when working through grief. Actions also express a person's thoughts.	The children danced and sang, "We love you, Grandpa."	Draw beautiful butterflies and hang them from the ceiling of the classroom or the library. Younger children can draw or paint pre-formed butterflies. Older students may draw butterflies freehand. Involve the participation of the art teacher. Ask the gym teacher to help in using interpretive dance to describe the stages of a butterfly's life cycle.	What can you do to show you remember someone special?
Gratitude	Grandparents teach many things for which grandchildren are grateful. How can grandchildren express that gratitude?	The children are grateful for all of the special qualities of their grandfather: their time with him in the garden, sitting on his lap and listening to him read, and watching him wink at them.	Talk about something special that the students' grandmothers or grandfathers taught them to do, and reinforce cherishing that special memory. Maybe it was to learn how to ride a bike, how to cook a favorite dish, or how to speak another language. Students may write a thank-you note to a grandparent for teaching them a special skill.	How are Holly and Glen remembering their grandfather?
Celebrating All of Life's Stages	One should not take special times with loved ones for granted.	The children celebrated the life of their grandfather. Holly and Glen will always remember him in a special way.	Draw a picture of an activity that you used to do with your special person, such as gardening or fishing.	Can you make a special dish with your family and then share it with your classmates? Can you read a favorite story that you used to enjoy together?

Book Hop

The Very Hungry Caterpillar by Eric Carle.
Philomel, 1994 (25th anniversary edition). ISBN: 0399227539. Unpaginated.
Grades: PreK–1.

A very hungry little caterpillar eats his way through a large amount of food. When he is full, he forms a cocoon around himself and goes to sleep until he becomes a beautiful butterfly.

Classic Corner

Charlotte's Web by E. B. White; illustrated by Garth Williams.
Harper & Row, 1952 (1st edition). ISBN: 0899666965. 184 pages.
Grades: All.

This is a classic story about the life cycle of Charlotte the Spider and her special bond with Wilbur the Pig. They live on the Arable farm, where daughter Fern cares for them. Charlotte spins words in her web and saves Wilbur's life.

For Older Children

Blackberries in the Dark by Mavis Jukes; illustrated by Thomas B. Allen.
Knopf, 1985. ISBN: 0394875990. 48 pages.
Grades: 2–4.

Austin is a nine-year-old boy who goes to visit his grandmother after his grandfather's death. The last time they were together, the boy and his grandpa picked blackberries in the dark and then the grandmother baked a pie, which they enjoyed during the nighttime.

Support Material for *Remember the Butterflies*

Awards and Honors
- Outstanding Science Trade Books for Children, National Science Teachers: 1991
- Kentucky Bluegrass Award Nominee: 1992
- *Baker & Taylor School Selection Guide K–8 Titles to Order*: 1992–95
- *Best Books for Children*, 5th edition: 1995

Reviews
- *School Library Journal*: May 1, 1991

CHAPTER **13**

Fires and Homelessness

13.1

Hero Cat by Eileen Spinelli; illustrated by Jo Ellen McAllister Stammen.
Marshall Cavendish, 2006. ISBN: 0761452230. 32 pages.
Grades: K–3.

Synopsis
Hero Cat is based on a true story of a homeless cat who daringly rescues and saves her kittens from an abandoned building that catches fire while she is out searching for food.

Booktalk
A mother cat gives birth to her litter in an abandoned building. In spite of being homeless, she cares for her kittens the best way she can. She nurses, cuddles, purrs, and licks them clean. When she returns from seeking food, she finds the building in flames. One by one, the mama cat saves all of her babies. In this true story, how do you think the mama cat dealt with her homeless situation? How did she react to the fire? Do you think we can call her a hero?

Shelf-Esteem Connection
Even a frightening fire will not affect a mother cat's instincts to save her kittens. Mothers sometimes perform heroic deeds when caring for their children.

THEME	MESSAGE	PLOT POINT CONNECTION	REINFORCING ACTIVITY	DISCUSSION QUESTIONS
Caring Mothers	No matter what, a mother cares for her young.	"Mother cat nursed and cuddled them. She purred starry lullabies and licked clean their silky fur."	Write down or draw a picture about how you would care for a cat and her kittens.	What are some ways mother cat could have provided food for her kittens?

(Cont'd.)

THEME	MESSAGE	PLOT POINT CONNECTION	REINFORCING ACTIVITY	DISCUSSION QUESTIONS
Unexpected Heroes	There are many types of heroes, including animals or children.	Hero Cat rose to the occasion and rescued her kittens because she found strength and courage that she did not know she had.	Make a chart of people or pets that you consider to be heroes. Explain what kind of heroic deeds they performed.	What kinds of deeds do heroes perform? What have you done that could be considered heroic? What is the difference between a small heroic deed and a bigger one?
Adopting a Pet	Shelters have many homeless pets that need good homes.	When the fireman found the kittens, he made sure that they were brought to an animal shelter and then adopted into caring homes.	Write a short article about Hero Cat and her kittens as if you were the reporter for the newspaper.	Why or why not would you like to adopt one of the kittens? How would you care for them?
Individuality	Every animal and every person is unique.	When mother cat gives birth to the kittens, they each have distinct colors and markings.	Draw or paint a picture of the five different kittens. Each one is an individual.	What qualities about you make you an individual? How would you describe yourself as different (or alike) from your brothers and sisters?
Lullabies	It seems that even kittens like to hear lullabies before falling off to sleep.	Mother cat purred lullabies to the kittens.	Write a poem or short lullaby that you would sing to the kittens.	What are you favorite lullabies? Look in some books in the library for lullabies that you could sing to your siblings.

Book Hop

Cats to the Rescue: True Tales of Heroic Felines by Marilyn Singer;
illustrated by Jean Cassels.
Henry Holt, 2006. ISBN: 0805074333. 154 pages.
Grades: 3 and up.

This book tells true stories of cats who have exhibited heroic or unusual behavior.

Classic Corner

Poinsettia and the Firefighters by Felicia Bond.
Thomas Y. Crowell, 1984. ISBN: 0060535091. 32 pages.
Grades: PreK–2.

Poinsettia is a pig who is frightened of the dark and being in her new home alone at night. She spots a fire on the telephone wire in front of her house and is comforted to know that firefighters stay awake all night to provide for her safety.

For Older Children

New York's Bravest by Mary Pope Osbourne; illustrated by Steve Johnson and Lou Fancher.
Knopf, 2002. ISBN: 0375821961. Unpaginated.
Grades: K–3.

Mose Humphrey was a real nineteenth-century New York firefighter who never hesitated to rush into a burning building to save lives. He became a legend—reminiscent of the heroes of 9-11 in New York City. The author speaks about Mose as America's first "urban folk hero."

Support Material for *Hero Cat*

Reviews
- *Booklist*: March 1, 2006.
- *School Library Journal*: April 1, 2006.

13.2

Fly Away Home by Eve Bunting; illustrated by Ronald Himler.
Clarion, 1991. ISBN: 0395559626. 32 pages.
Grades: K–5.

Synopsis

Andrew, a homeless boy who lives with his father at the airport, moves from terminal to terminal to remain inconspicuous. One day he notices a bird trapped in the terminal, and he sees its eventual release as a sign of hope for the future.

Booktalk

Do you think it is fun to go to the airport? Do you think it would still be fun if you had no choice but to live at the airport? Andrew and his father move to the airport when they become homeless. His dad wanted a place where they would be safe until they had enough money to move into a new house or apartment again. Not only is it not much fun, but it is against the law. They move around to different places in the airport so they do not get caught. They wash up in the mornings in the airport bathrooms and buy food at the cafeteria with what little money they do have. On the weekends, Andrew stays with another homeless family in the airport when his father goes to work. One day, Andrew spots a bird trying to flee from the airport. He knows somehow they both will escape their trapped situation. Andrew tells the bird to never give up.

Shelf-Esteem Connection

People who do not have homes or have other problems in life are having a very difficult time and often feel helpless. One should feel compassion for them.

THEME	MESSAGE	PLOT POINT CONNECTION	REINFORCING ACTIVITY	DISCUSSION QUESTIONS
Empathy	Having empathy for people who are less fortunate is an admirable trait.	Sometimes Andrew gets mad, and sometimes he feels jealous. He feels angry about being in a helpless situation and mad because the other people he sees have houses to which they are returning.	Divide a paper into thirds. Label the first third Anger, the next third Jealousy, and the final third Feeling Sad. Draw a picture showing how the main characters experience each of these emotions.	How do you feel about Andrew's loss of his home and the loss of his mother? What would you miss the most if you had to live in an airport like Andrew and his father do?

(Cont'd.)

THEME	MESSAGE	PLOT POINT CONNECTION	REINFORCING ACTIVITY	DISCUSSION QUESTIONS
Changing Attitudes	It is best to try to look for things that will bring happiness and optimism, no matter what is happening at the time.	Andrew shows hope for the future by being optimistic; i.e., looking on the bright side of situations.	*Librarian:* Ask the younger children to dictate a paragraph or two telling why Andrew can be happier when he is thinking about the future. Older children will be able to write their own paragraphs.	How can Andrew help himself feel better?
Hope	There is hope even in the direst of circumstances.	Seeing the bird finally fly off and become free made Andrew so happy. Dad tells Andrew that when he gets more work and he saves some money, they will be able to have their own apartment again.	Imagine Andrew with wings trying to escape his bad situation. Draw a picture of him leaving the airport.	Why did the bird make Andrew so happy? How do you think Andrew felt when the bird flew off and was free?
Solving Problems	People who find themselves homeless or without income want to move on to a new life.	Andrew no longer has a mother, and he no longer has a home. But he still wants to go back to a normal life. One of the things he does to help is to save some money by hiding it in his shoe.	Taking action is one way to help yourself get out of a bad situation. Make a list of ways Andrew and his father can earn money to try to help themselves move on to a new life.	How can Andrew and his father help themselves?
Solving Problems	Actively doing something to improve a situation makes a person feel better and come closer to his or her goal.	Andrew wants his father to know that he feels the need to do something to help change his situation.	Make up an action plan for Andrew and his father to help them move from their makeshift home in the airport so that they can become free, just like the bird. *Librarian:* Stress the need for personal strength and resilience during challenging times of life.	How does Andrew's hiding money in his shoe help him feel that he is doing something to help solve the problem of homelessness?

Book Hop

I Can Hear the Sun: A Modern Myth by Patricia Polacco.
Philomel, 1996. ISBN: 039922520X. Unpaginated.
Grades: K–3.

Park-keeper Stephanie Michelle cares for the animals and some homeless people on Merritt Lake. She introduces Fondo, a homeless boy, to a blind goose. Fondo's wish is to be magically transformed into a goose and be invited to fly away to freedom.

Classic Corner

A Chance to Shine by Steve Seskin and Allen Shamblin;
illustrated by R. Gregory Christie.
Tricycle, 2005. ISBN: 1582461678. 32 pages.
Grades: PreK–3.

This book takes the lyrics of a song written by the authors in 1991 about a dad who offers a homeless man a chance at life by giving him work. The lyrics sing out: "Every heart needs a chance to shine/to be wanted by someone somewhere down the line." The boy learns by his father's example of generosity and tolerance.

For Older Children

Talk and write about the importance of having hope for the future and being optimistic: i.e., looking on the bright side of situations.

Support Material for *Fly Away Home*

Awards and Honors
- National Association of Parenting Publications Awards Winner: 1991
- ALA Best First Novels for Youth: 1991
- California. Book Awards Winner: 1991
- International Reading Association, Teacher's Choice: 1992
- *Baker & Taylor School Selection Guide K–8 Titles to Order*: 1994–99
- *Best Books For Children*, 6th edition: 1998
- Maryland Black-Eyed Susan Picture Books Nominations: 1992–93
- Pennsylvania Young Readers Choice Books (Elementary): 1994–95
- Picture Books to Enhance the Curriculum: 1996
- Reading Rainbow Guide to Children's Books, The 100 Best Titles: 1994
- Tennessee Volunteer State Book Awards, Primary: 1994–95

Reviews
- *Kirkus*: February 15, 1991
- *Publishers Weekly*: March 29, 1993

13.3

Smoky Night by Eve Bunting; illustrated by David Diaz.
Harcourt Brace, 1994. ISBN: 0152699546. Unpaginated.
Grades: K–4.

Synopsis

The streets of Los Angeles, California, break out in riots and the houses are all set on fire. People, steal, loot, and rob. Daniel and his mother go to a shelter for safety and find that their missing cat, Jasmine, has been rescued by a firefighter. The boy and his mom learn the value of getting along with others no matter what their background or nationality.

Booktalk

Rioters are breaking windows and setting fires. Daniel and his mother escape to a shelter where they can feel safe. How would you feel if your neighborhood was on fire—threatened by people who "want to smash and destroy and don't care about right and wrong?"

Shelf-Esteem Connection

There is utmost value in trying to get along with all peoples. Frustration and anger on the part of adults can be difficult and scary for children to handle.

THEME	MESSAGE	PLOT POINT CONNECTION	REINFORCING ACTIVITY	DISCUSSION QUESTIONS
Safety with Family	The safest place to be in a time of uncertainly or danger is with family members.	Daniel stays close by his mother's side when violence erupts in his neighborhood. She comforts him through the chaos.	Write or dictate a paragraph about a time when you felt scared and someone in your family offered comforting words.	Why is it important to stay close to family during uncertain times?
Dealing with Uncertainty	When people ignore what is right and wrong it is almost impossible to understand what is happening.	Daniel holds his cat for safety and security. He doesn't understand the rioting and the stealing.	Describe how you would find safety and security if your neighborhood were threatened.	How did holding Jasmine help Daniel through an uncertain, confusing time?
Community	People tend to help each other in times of emergency.	The people in the neighborhood band together and seek the safety of a shelter. They discuss what happened and agreed that it was a "sad, sad night."	Write or draw about a time when other people helped you through a tough situation.	How did being together and talking about the problem help the people in the community?
Hope for the Future	There is always some reason for hope.	The cats lived through the dark night, and there is hope for their future. The fires were put out in Daniel's building and he will be able to return home soon.	Gena Kim invites Daniel and his cat over to her house after things settle down. What constructive things can Gena Kim and Daniel do together to help the healing process?	Something good came out of something bad. Hope for the future is most important. What words can you think of that mean hope? Can you find the word hope translated into other languages?
Getting to Know Each Other	Sometimes people think they don't like each other because they really don't know each other.	The cats found out about each other and learned that they could get along. Mama had thought they didn't like each other, but the fact was that they didn't know each other before.	Write or draw a picture about someone or something that you thought you didn't like, but then when you learned more about it, you started to under-stand it and like it more.	What did you not like at first? When you gave something a chance, did you find you enjoyed it? It might be a food, a pet, or even a person. How did Daniel and his cat make a new friend?

Book Hop

Officer Buckle and Gloria by Peggy Rathmann.
G.P. Putnam's Sons, 1995. ISBN: 0399226168. Unpaginated.
Grades: K–3.

In this Caldecott Medal-winning book, Officer Buckle and his sidekick dog, Gloria, offer safety tips in a humorous fashion. There are many important words of advice on keeping safe on the endpapers of the book.

Classic Corner

Prayer for a Child by Rachel Field; illustrated by Elizabeth Orton Jones.
Aladdin, 1973. ISBN: 0020430701. Unpaginated.
Grades: K–2.

This Caldecott Medal winner offers gratitude prayers for children everywhere.

For Older Children

The Heart of the City by Ronald Koertge.
Orchard, 1998. ISBN: 0531330788. 137 pages.
Grades: 4-7.

Ten-year-old Joy Fontaine and her parents move from the suburbs to Los Angeles. Joy befriends Neesha, and the two of them work to restore the safety of their neighborhood through cooperation and tolerance.

Support Material for *Smoky Night*

Awards and Honors
• National Council of Teachers of English, *Adventuring with Books: A Booklist for PreK–Grade 6*: 1997
• ALSC American Library Association, *The American Experience: Strength from Diversity*: 1995
• *Children's Catalog*, 18th edition: 2001
• National Council of Teachers of English, *Kaleidoscope, a Multicultural Booklist for Grades K–8*, 2nd edition: 1997.
• California Book Awards Winner, Ages up to 10: 1994.
• Children's Literature Council of Southern California Awards, Distinguished Picture Book: 1995.
• Kentucky Bluegrass Award Nominee: 1996
• Randolph Caldecott Medal: David Diaz, illustrator, 1995
• *School Library Journal* Best Book of the Year: 1994

Reviews
• *Kirkus* Book Review Stars: 1994
• *Publishers Weekly* Book Review Stars: 1994
• *Horn Book*: Fall 1994
• *Booklist*: March 1, 1994
• *Bulletin of the Center for Children's Books*: March 1994

Chapter 14

Divorce

14.1

Always My Dad by Sharon Dennis Wyeth; illustrated by Raul Colon.
Knopf, 1995. ISBN: 0679934472. 32 pages.
Grades: PreK–3.

Synopsis

Although she does not get to see her father very often, a girl enjoys the time she and her brothers spend with him one summer while they are visiting their grandparents' farm. Based on her own memories of her summer visits with her father at her grandparents' farm in Virginia, Sharon Dennis Wyeth evokes the love between a daughter and her absentee father. She understands that he will always be her father and he will always love her. Meanwhile, she develops a stronger relationship with her grandparents and siblings to compensate for not seeing her father as often as she would like.

Booktalk (Narrative)

"I only see my dad once in a while and sometimes he's the person I want to see more than anyone else in the world. I know Dad tells me he is "having a problem getting his life together" and to try to understand. We have fun when I see him at my grandparents. We brush our teeth outside at the pump, go barefoot, catch lightning bugs, and play games together. Even though I don't get to see my dad every day, I cherish the time I do get to spend with him."

Shelf-Esteem Connection

Parents love their children even when they are living away from the rest of the family.

THEME	MESSAGE	PLOT POINT CONNECTION	REINFORCING ACTIVITY	DISCUSSION QUESTIONS
Parental Love	Parental love is unconditional. A parent does not have to be a constant companion to love his or her children.	Dad says: "Just remember, wherever I am, I'm always your dad."	Write a letter to your dad telling him how much you care about him.	If you only got to see your dad every now and then, (like the girl in the book) what questions would you want to ask him?

THEME	MESSAGE	PLOT POINT CONNECTION	REINFORCING ACTIVITY	DISCUSSION QUESTIONS
Extended Families	Grandparents and siblings, aunts and uncles provide a solid foundation for children whose parents are absent.	The girl forges a stronger relationship with her grandparents and her siblings and even her favorite horse, Sir Imp, to make up for the loss of the father figure in her life.	Draw a picture of your family circle and label each person in it that you can turn to for support.	Whom would you want to visit if you were the girl in this story?
Quality Rather Than Quantity	You do not have to see someone often to have special times with that person.	The protagonist doesn't get to see her dad ever day. She makes the times she *does* see him really count.	Make a list of special activities you like to do with your dad. Do you do these things every day or just once in a while?	What activities do you like to do with your dad? What do you wish you could do?
Changing Attitudes by Helping	Even if you are disappointed about something, helping others may be interesting and fun.	Even though the girl was disappointed at first that dad was not with her on the farm, she kept busy by helping Grandpa weed the vegetable garden and helped Grandma pick blackberries in the woods.	Draw a picture of how you help out at home or at your grandparents' house.	What would you do to help yourself feel better if you were disappointed about something?
Holding on to Your Dreams	Your dreams can give you strength and hope. Even if you know it is a dream, you can still have faith and believe in it.	The girl talks about a dream she has where she is standing in a field with her dad and lots of stars are in the sky. She sees an orange-colored sweet potato moon, and candle flies fluttering all around.	On one side of a paper, draw a picture of the girl's dream. On the other side, draw something that you wish for too.	What would be your wish for the girl and her father?

Book Hop

At Daddy's on Saturdays by Linda Walvoord Girard; illustrated by Judith Friedman.
Albert Whitman, 1987. ISBN: 0807504750. 32 pages.
Grades: K–2.

This book brings to the surface the confusion, the concern, and the sadness a young girl feels when her parents divorce and her father moves away. Katie's mom reassures her that dad will come back, but not every day. Katie and her dad make up a calendar to schedule visits together, which occur on Saturdays and Sundays, "not every week, but often."

Classic Corner

Sometimes Mama and Papa Fight by Marjorie Weinman Sharmat; illustrated by Kay Choras.
Harper & Row, 1980. ISBN: 0060256117. 30 pages.
Grades: PreK–2.

Kevin and Millicent hate when their parents fight. They try everything they can to get them to stop—they whistle, sing, and try to think about other things. Although seeing parents fight can be very scary, Kevin and Millicent come to understand that fighting is a natural part of being in a family, and that when the fights are resolved, life goes on.

For Older Children

When dad and the children play "devil and pies," he decides which child represents which secret flavor. Decide what type of pie you would like to be and write down why you would like to be that type of pie.

Support Material for *Always My Dad*

Awards and Honors
- Texas Reading Club: 1999
- *Baker & Taylor School Selection Guide K–8 Titles to Order*: 1997–99
- *Children's Catalog*, 17th edition: 1996
- *Connecting Cultures*, Guide to Multicultural Literature for Childen: 1996
- A Reading Rainbow Book

Reviews
- *Booklist*: February 15, 1995
- *Horn Book*: Fall 1995
- *Kirkus* Starred Review: January 1, 1995
- *School Library Journal*: December 1, 1995
- *Bulletin of the Center for Children's Books*: February 1995
- *New York Times Book Review*: April 23, 1995

14.2

Getting Used to Harry by Cari Best; illustrated by Diane Palmisciano.
Orchard, 1996. ISBN: 0531094944. Unpaginated.
Grades: PreK–3.

Synopsis

Cynthia's mother is remarrying; the man is named Harry. At first, Cynthia can't seem to adjust to the subsequent changes in her life at home. Eventually, she finds that as she spends time with Harry, opening her heart and mind, she can get used to life with her mother's new husband.

Booktalk (Narrative)

"Do you think I will ever get used to this stranger living with my mom and me? It wasn't that long ago that he was just Harry, the shoe store man. I guess he's not really a stranger; he married my mom, and moved into our house. Things have changed around our house. We don't eat plain pasta like we used to. Mom's always dancing with Harry, too. But one night, when I couldn't sleep, Harry took me for a 'flashlight walk.' Once he showed me his trick with marbles. He even let me change his window display at the shoe store. I think I'm getting used to Harry after all."

Shelf-Esteem Connection

Change is inevitable but often difficult. Children and adults eventually learn to accept change and move on.

THEME	MESSAGE	PLOT POINT CONNECTION	REINFORCING ACTIVITY	DISCUSSION QUESTIONS
Adjusting to Change	When a mother remarries, a child has to adjust to her mother and stepfather doing things themselves.	When Inky and Harry went off on their honeymoon, Cynthia stayed with her grandmother and played games.	Make a list or draw a picture of the kinds of games you would prefer to play with your grandparents, aunts, or uncles.	What kinds of questions would you like to ask Harry to get to know him better?
Self-Soothers	Sometimes people have to find their own ways of making themselves feel better.	When Cynthia has trouble falling asleep, she tries a variety of methods to soothe herself: reading a book, shooting imaginary marbles, and even counting her teeth (instead of sheep).	Describe in words and pictures what you do when you have trouble falling asleep. You can also write a poem or haiku about it.	What could you do if you are having trouble falling asleep?
Adjusting to Change	It is not easy for Cynthia to adjust to a new adult living in her house.	Cynthia is not sure she likes the new arrangement at her house. But she tries to adjust by playing games with her grandma.	Write about what Cynthia does to try to cope with the changes going on around her.	If you were Cynthia's friend, how could you help her?
Spending Time Together	Cynthia really gets to know Harry better after he spends some concentrated time with her.	When Harry can't sleep, he goes for a walk with a flashlight. During that walk, Cynthia and Harry get to know each other better through spending time with each other.	Go for a "flashlight walk" in the classroom or library. Shut the lights and the shades and see what books you can find.	Does getting to know someone better help you feel more comfortable with him or her? What are some ways to get to know someone better?
Accepting People	Accepting new people takes time and effort in order to get to know them.	Harry made Cynthia feel included in his life by spending more time with her and getting to know her. Harry told her that he knew she liked marbles and that she liked shoes.	Pair off with someone else in the room and ask about that person's interests. When you pay attention to someone, it shows you care about them. Make of list of their likes and dislikes.	Did Cynthia feel better about Harry after she spent some more time with him?

Book Hop

My Wicked Stepmother by Norman Leach; illustrated by Jane Browne.
Macmillan, 1993. ISBN: 0027547000. Unpaginated.
Grades: PreK–2.

When his father remarries, seven-year-old Tom has trouble accepting his new stepmother. Tom eventually learns to adjust to his new stepmother after a rocky start.

Classic Corner

My Mother's House, My Father's House by C.B. Christiansen; illustrated by Irene Trivas. Atheneum, 1989. ISBN: 0689313942. Unpaginated.
Grades: PreK–2.

Empathize with a girl who has divorced parents and how she handles living with her mom during the week and with her dad on the weekends. She fantasizes about living in one house with both parents together.

For Older Children

The author uses a literary device called "alliteration," which is a series of words that start with the same letter. Examine the alliteration in these sentences: "Harry was standing, sitting, slipping and sneezing and Cynthia was washing, whistling, waiting, and watching." Go through the illustrations and words in this book and find more examples of words that start with the same letters, one after the other, to show alliteration.

Support Material for *Getting Used to Harry*

Awards and Honors
- *Baker & Taylor School Selection Guide K–8 Titles to Order*: 1998–99
- Best Books for Children, 6th and 7th editions: 1998, 2002

Reviews
- *Booklist*: November 1, 1996
- *Bulletin of the Center for Children's Books* Recommended Titles: 1996
- *Horn Book*: Spring 1997
- *Kirkus*: August 15, 1996
- *School Library Journal*: October 1, 1996

CHAPTER 15

Separation Anxiety

15.1

Don't Forget to Come Back! by Robie H. Harris; illustrated by Harry Bliss.
Candlewick, 2004. ISBN: 0763617822. Unpaginated.
Grades: PreK–2.

Synopsis
When her parents go out for the evening, a little girl threatens to run off to Alaska. Instead she has a good time with the babysitter.

Booktalk
What stalling tactics would you use if you didn't want your parents to go out for the evening? The girl in this story tries her best to get her parents to change their minds about going out and leaving her with a babysitter. But no matter what she says or does, her parents still do go out. Will the girl have a great time with Sarah, the babysitter?

Shelf- Esteem Connection
Learning to adjust to parental separations is a difficult task young children face, but self-reliance and trust will help children deal with the separation and their fears.

THEME	MESSAGE	PLOT POINT CONNECTION	REINFORCING ACTIVITY	DISCUSSION QUESTIONS
Positive Thinking	Staying with a babysitter can be a positive experience.	The baby sitter makes pizza and paints the girl's fingernails with silver and purple polish.	Draw a picture of the kinds of food you would like to prepare with a baby sitter.	What activity would you choose to do with a baby-sitter?
New Experiences	Family members or other caretakers can expand a child's wealth of experience.	The parents in his book cannot take their daughter out with them. Children can stay with grandparents or babysitters until their parents come home.	Make a list of fun activities you can do with a caretaker until mom and dad get back.	Who would you choose to spend time with if your parents needed to go out?

(Cont'd.)

THEME	MESSAGE	PLOT POINT CONNECTION	REINFORCING ACTIVITY	DISCUSSION QUESTIONS
Trust	Parents go out, but they also come back home.	In this book, when Mom and Dad are getting ready to go out, readers can see paintings in the hallway of their house. These paintings are significant because they offer a sense of place and security.	Notice the details in the illustrations. Choose one of the paintings and decide why you think this particular painting is on display in the house.	Why do think the painting of the penguins is shown? Does it have anything to do with the girl's desire to go to the South Pole?
Repetition	Repetition brings security.	Sarah reads the girl's book to her five times in a row.	If you were feeling anxious, there are some activities that would probably comfort you. Make a list of things you could do over and over again that would make you feel better about a situation.	What questions would you like to ask your parents before they go out?
Self-reliance	Trusting in onerself and in loved ones can help a person rely on inner strength.	The girl in this story is always telling her parents three important things. She wants her parents to pay attention to her and to trust her, and she wants to learn to trust them.	Write or dictate a list of three important things to tell your parents before they go out for the evening. What do you want them to know?	What would you like to tell your parents to remember while they are out? Would you want them to call you? Would you want to know when they will be back?

Book Hop

Even If I Spill My Milk? by Anna Grossnickle Hines.
Clarion, 1994. ISBN: 0395650100. 32 pages.
Grades: PreK–2.

A young child uses stalling tactics to keep his parents at home just a little while longer.

Classic Corner

The Goodbye Book by Judith Viorst; illustrated by Kay Chorao.
Atheneum, 1988. ISBN: 068931308X. Unpaginated.
Grades: PreK–2.

A boy doesn't want his parents to go out and he doesn't want to be left behind. He invents many tactics to make his parents stay at home. He feigns sickness, asks to hear another story, and then he threatens not to listen to the story anyway. It turns out his babysistter is a wonderful storyteller, and he is finally able to separate from his parents for a while.

For Older Children

The protagonist would feel better if she knew just where her parents were going, what they were going to do when they got there, and when they would be home. Make up a schedule or a clock that would represent the parents' activities and timetable for when they will leave, what they will do while they are out, and when they will be back at home. Knowledge brings confidence, security, and power. Power brings a sense of control.

Support Material for *Don't Forget to Come Back!*

Awards and Honors
- Bank Street College of Education, *Best Children's Books of the Year*: 2004
- International Reading Association, *Children's Choices*: 2005

Reviews
- *Horn Book*: Fall 2004
- *Kirkus*: January 1, 2004
- *Publishers Weekly*: February 2, 2004
- *School Library Journal*: March 1, 2004
- *New York Times Book Review*: June 6, 2004

15.2

The Stars Will Still Shine by Cynthia Rylant; illustrated by Tiphanie Beeke.

HarperCollins, 2005. ISBN: 0060546395. Unpaginated.
Grades: PreK–1.

Synopsis

In uncertain times, it is reassuring to hear the soothing words of author Cynthia Rylant as she recounts the numerous ways people can feel secure and comforted by the familiar. This tale offers an opportunity for children to express gratitude for the certain and comforting aspects of their lives. In pictures and rhyming text, this verse reassures the reader that life's familiar things, such as stars that shine and sleeping kittens, will always be there.

Booktalk

What are the things in your life that you take for granted? What things or people are there for you every day? Do you take time to notice or thank them each day for being there? In this book, the narrator is thankful for the birds that fly in the sky, the flowers that bloom in every spring, peaches and ice cream in the summertime, and a warm home to return to each day.

Shelf-Esteem Connection

One way to combat separation anxiety is to build confidence in one's ability to stay alone. Acknowledging the comfort we receive from the known and familiar aspects of everyday life is a big step.

THEME	MESSAGE	PLOT POINT CONNECTION	REINFORCING ACTIVITY	DISCUSSION QUESTIONS
Gratitude	Gratitude helps us keep focused on the good things in life.	One of the things the characters are grateful for is having family meals together.	Write or dictate a list of things you are grateful to have in your life each day. Then draw a picture of	If you were planning a meal, what would the menu look like? What are some of the

(Cont'd.)

THEME	MESSAGE	PLOT POINT CONNECTION	REINFORCING ACTIVITY	DISCUSSION QUESTIONS
Gratitude (Cont'd.)			them or bring in photos for an album. You might create a "Stars Will Still Shine" booklet for your own days. It can start with "I get up in the morning. I am happy to have cereal for my breakfast. Then I go to school where my teacher is waiting for me."	things that we count on being there day after day—like sunshine or the stars shining in the sky?
Taking Things for Granted	It is possible to learn to be more conscious and take notice of the things one takes for granted each day.	The cover of the book shows a mom reading to her two children before bedtime. We know it is nighttime because we see the moon and the stars. The moon is always out at night, but it always changes. Some nights it is just a sliver; other nights, there will be a full moon.	Draw a picture of the different ways the moon can look at night. Discuss how even though the moon is out at night, it still changes.	Even though we can't always see the moon because of clouds in the sky, do we know if it is still there? How do we know the moon is there even when we can't see it?
Accepting Change	Change is inevitable, even though many things stay the same.	The stories you hear each night may be different, but you can count on being read to each night, just like the picture on the cover of the book.	Make a list of the different people who read stories to you. You are being read to, but the person who reads may change.	Can you think of something that has changed for you at home or at school?
Making Things from Raw Materials	Things do not create themselves. People work to make things from raw materials.	The author writes the following: "We shall have peaches . . . we shall have pie." The peaches will change into peach pie only if we do the work ourselves.	List the steps required to make a peach pie. Make a "pretend" pie out of play-doh or clay.	Does this book make you notice some things that you didn't pay attention to before?
The Rhythm of Our Days	There are certain things that happen each day that provide structure and security.	The book has a certain rhythm because we come to know what to expect next. It gives us comfort and warm, fuzzy feelings.	Make a list of things or people you can count on each day to be there for you. It might be a teacher, a crossing guard, a policeman, a relative, a friend, a sibling, parents, or grandparents.	Does this book make you feel different about what you see and do every day?

Book Hop

I Love You, Little One by Nancy Tafuri.
Scholastic, 1998. ISBN: 0590921592. Unpaginated.
Grades: PreK–1.

A deer, a duck, a rabbit, and a child ask their mothers for reassurance and love. The Mamas each answer with warmth and devotion.

Classic Corner

The Runaway Bunny by Margaret Wise Brown; pictures by Clement Hurd.
HarperCollins, 2005 (60th anniversary edition). ISBN: 0060775831. Unpaginated.
Grades: PreK–1.

In this classic tale, the bunny receives the ultimate reassurance from his mother about her continuous love,which comforts him and gives him security.

For Older Children

Since this book is told in rhyming words, such as shine and chime, sleep and keep, try to think of some more rhyming words (For example: teacher/preacher, friend/pretend).

Support Materials for *The Stars Will Still Shine*

Awards and Honors
• *Books for Growing Minds*: September 2005

Reviews
• *Booklist*: October 15, 2005
• *Bulletin of the Center for Children's Books*: January 2006
• *Horn Book*: Spring 2006
• *Kirkus*: October 1, 2005
• *School Library Journal*: October 1, 2005
• *New York Times Book Review*: November 13, 2005

15.3

While You Are Away by Eileen Spinelli; illustrated by Renée Graef.
Hyperion, 2004. ISBN: 0786809728. Unpaginated.
Grades: PreK–2.

Synopsis

Three children of different ethnicities each have a parent who serves in the military, which disrupts their lives. A white girl's mother is off flying planes, an African-American boy's father is away on a ship, and a Latino boy's father is driving a jeep. The children describe how they feel when one of their parents is away.

Booktalk

How do we stay close to the people we love when they are away? Sometimes we feel sad when our moms or dads have to leave home because of their jobs. One little boy wonders about his father's life in the Navy. What does he eat for breakfast? Where does he sleep? Is he feeling well? The boy sends his dad a package to feel closer. What could you do if your mom or dad were in the military and had to live far away from you?

Shelf-Esteem Connection

It is difficult for children to deal with an absentee parent for whatever reason. Thinking of ways to stay connected will help ease anxieties.

THEME	MESSAGE	PLOT POINT CONNECTION	REINFORCING ACTIVITY	DISCUSSION QUESTIONS
Staying Connected	There are many ways to stay in touch with parents, wherever they might be.	The children in this book are wondering about their parents who are far away from home.	Write a letter to dad as if you were the character in the book. Ask any questions you may have about what he is doing while he is away. Talk about what you might have put in a package to send to him and why you sent it.	What ways could you think of to stay in contact with a parent who was far away?
Staying Focused	Thinking positively and keeping a goal in mind can help overcome anxieties and fears.	The little girl in this book has a dream of carrying a red balloon when her mom comes home.	Draw a picture of your dreams and what you would wish for if your parent were far away.	What would your dream of a reunion be?
Helping Out	Being responsible for something helps children feel empowered and being helpful gives them self-esteem.	A boy in the story tends to his papa's garden while Papa is away. He pulls weeds, waters the plants, and paints the fence.	Draw a picture of what you could do to help around the house.	How can you help around your house?
Looking toward the Future	Dreams and expectations can help carry a person through some lonely times.	The boy feels so thrilled when the day finally comes when his papa arrives back home. He says it is the day to turn cartwheels across the living room floor, the day to laugh till his tummy aches, and the day to cry a cereal-bowl full of happy tears.	Think of what you would do and draw a picture to celebrate the homecoming. Use words to describe the way you would feel if your parent had just arrived home after being away for a long time. Turn those words into a poem.	How do you picture the homecoming? What would you look forward to the most?
Hope	Being filled with hope keeps up a person's spirits.	The boy waters the cilantro, which is an herb that is grown in a garden. By taking responsibility for the plants, he is helping to keep busy, and he has a productive, hopeful attitude.	*Librarian:* Bring in cilantro from the store or farm so that the children can smell the herb. Write about their reactions to the herb's smell.	What would you plant in your garden?

Book Hop

Home to Me, Home to You by Jennifer A. Ericsson; illustrated by Ashley Wolff.
Little, Brown, 2005. ISBN: 0316609226. Unpaginated.
Grades: PreK–2.

A child is separated from her mother while the mother is on a business trip. Finally the mother returns, and the two are reunited.

Classic Corner

Daddy, Will You Miss Me? by Wendy McCormick; illustrated by Jennifer Eachus.
Simon & Schuster, 1999. ISBN: 068981898X. 32 pages.
Grades: PreK–2.

The narrator is waiting for his dad to return home from a business trip to Africa. After a month's time, he reunites with his dad after sending kisses across the ocean and keeping track of the days passing using a calendar.

For Older Children

When's Dad's at Sea by Mindy L. Pelton; illustrated by Robert Gantt Steele.
Albert Whitman, 2004. ISBN: 0807563390. 32 pages.
Grades: 1–3.

Emily's dad is a Navy pilot, and he will be away on an aircraft carrier for six months time. A piece of paper chain is torn off for each day that he is gone. Emily finds where her dad is located by consulting a map. She is able to send him e-mails and call him to make the time seem shorter until he returns home.

Support Material for *While You Are Away*

Awards and Honors
- *School Selection Guide Core Issue: All Titles K–6*: 2005–06
- *Books and More for Growing Minds*: March 2004

Reviews
- *Booklist*: March 15, 2004
- *Horn Book*: Fall 2004
- *Kirkus*: March 1, 2004
- *School Library Journal*: April 1, 2004

PART II

Shelf-Esteem
Essentials

CHAPTER 16
======

Exploring the Shelf-Esteem Concept

WHAT IS SHELF-ESTEEM?

Self-esteem has been called the "confidence in our ability to cope with the challenges of life" (Branden, 1994). If you help a person develop this type of confidence through reading, you are helping that person develop *shelf*-esteem. Shelf-esteem is also the confidence that comes from becoming a budding lifelong reader as well as the confidence children gain from understanding what they read. By introducing children to an ever-widening circle of literature, we introduce them to the world in which they live and give them the resources they need to understand and cope with that world through background knowledge.

In the Shelf-Esteem program, the top priority for teachers and librarians is to develop and maintain the child's motivation to read. They recognize and praise each reading accomplishment, and, because each achievement builds on the previous one, every child will develop a sense of shelf-esteem.

The Shelf-Esteem approach to reading will empower both the reader and the educator, and children will be motivated to read books that speak to their passions, interests, and personal situations. Shelf-Esteem can be used as a tool for librarians and teachers to motivate students to read, to increase interest in the books they read, to fuel students' feelings of confidence in their ability to read, bolster self-esteem, and ultimately to instill a lifelong love of reading in children.

Using the principles of Shelf-Esteem helps children to:

- increase their knowledge and broaden their world, and thus feel better about themselves
- expand their comprehension skills and thus gain confidence
- increase their vocabulary exponentially and learn how to write by modeling other writers' techniques
- find solutions to their own problems by witnessing others in similar life situations, and identifying with characters who are "just like them"
- find heroines and heroes to emulate and model themselves after
- discover creative ways to solve problems

LEARNING TO COPE THROUGH SHELF-ESTEEM

The booktalks, activities, and discussions in the Shelf-Esteem program help youngsters become independent problem-solvers. Children will begin to be able to decide how to solve various problems for themselves based on the behavior of the characters in the books. Instead of being told what to do, they are given the freedom of discovering for themselves what the right course of action should be. This in itself is a valuable component of feeling competent and self-confident. Giving children the skills to solve problems on their own (or at least equipping them with models of behavior) is a very important gift that we can give to children via books.

There are several ways in which reading helps children to cope. Through reading, children

• learn to identify with others in a similar situation
• understand that they are not facing problems by themselves
• expand their understanding to encompass something new
• have the opportunity to experience catharsis
• gain insight into other's motivations, goals, and feelings
• ease their burdens with other points of view

ENCOURAGING MOTIVATION

If learners perceive tasks as interesting, personally relevant, and meaningful, then they will be intrinsically motivated to learn. It is up to the teacher or librarian to assess the difficulty of the task and match it to the learner's ability. This is because it is crucial for the child to believe that he or she can succeed in the task. If the task is related to the real world of the child and if the child is able to exert some control—that is, to exercise some degree of choice—then the child will want to make the effort.

The following criteria will help you to accurately evaluate a motivating activity for Shelf-Esteem:

1. The text should be personally relevant to the child.
2. The text should be of an appropriate complexity.
3. The task related to the book should be novel and interesting.
4. The student should believe in his or her ability to succeed, based on previous practice with the Shelf-Esteem model.
5. Students have to be given the opportunity to make their own choices for the process to work.

When you are reading a story aloud, ask children to put themselves in the character's place and decide what they would do next *before* you turn the page. Encourage suppositions, educated guesses, and predictions. The idea is for them to put themselves into the character's shoes. Have them talk and write about how the book made them feel. If they were put in the character's situation, do they think they would they have acted that same way or would they have done things differently? Writing a letter to the character will help them articulate their feelings.

KEY WAYS TO BUILD SHELF-ESTEEM

Build Shelf-Esteem: Top Tips

1. Help students identify and develop their reading strengths.
2. Give students opportunities to use their talents.
3. Give student's frequent positive feedback.
4. Show pride in your students' accomplishments by displaying their work on bulletin boards, newsletters, notes sent home, and online communications.
5. Put on your "sunshine glasses." There are always two ways to see everything, so look on the sunny side. Don't see a mistake as a failure. View it as a challenge and an opportunity to do better the next time. My daughter's science teacher called exams "Days of Opportunity: A chance to show the teacher how much you have learned." He said this was the students' chance to shine.

Make Reading Fun

To increase a child's interest in reading, it is important to make reading fun, to associate books with comfort, and to help children feel confident in their ability to read.

> What kids know:
>   Books in the Library = Knowledge
> What you want kids to learn:
>   Books in the Library = Comfort, Pleasure, Fun
>   Books in the Library = Confidence
>   Books in the Library = Shelf-Esteem

Alfred Mercier once said, "What we learn with pleasure we never forget." This holds for reading as well. Children are born to be receptive to enjoyment. "The most important thing you can do for your child is to make reading fun—not work" (Golinkoff, Hirsh-Pasek and Eyer, 2004: 99). Students are most receptive when they are having fun. That is why using puppetry, music, dance, jokes, reading scripts—anything that associates reading with enjoyment—will motivate and interest students and, thereby, raise their shelf-esteem. Teachers and librarians need to hone in on the fun aspects of reading, because what is fun and engaging is what children will remember.

Reading aloud will also help to make books more fun and will help children remember what they heard. When you read aloud and explain the text aloud to someone else, it reinforces the material in your own mind as well as benefiting the other person. Shelf-esteem is contagious—catch it and pass it on!

Make Reading Relaxing

Too often children are taught to read according to a set curriculum that does not take the individual child's interests or readiness into account. All children read the same book at the same time, and the only accommodations made for different abilities are the skill-based reading groups. However, children always know which groups are for the "good" readers and which are for the "slow" readers, and thus reading classes and library times become sources of stress rather than times for fun.

Children also tend to equate reading with getting ready for a test. However, if kids always associate reading with being judged and being tested, they will never develop that visceral response of

Books = Relaxation

To prepare children to be Shelf-Esteem readers, adult educators will want to shift the way individuals (you, the children, and their parents) think about text. Change their thinking from "Ugh—I *have* to read this" to "I *want* to read this." But to make that leap, students need positive connections to their reading experiences and reinforcement. Studies done over the past 20 years maintain that in order to be a motivated reader, one must first feel good about oneself as a reader, and then develop a positive relationship with books.

One major goal is to provide a complete and positive experience surrounding a student's relationship with reading. Your commitment to the children will ensure that the chosen books have deep meaning and interest to them, that the books match their reading levels, and that you (the librarian, teacher, or parent) will provide activities and experiences that will make that particular book-reading experience the most positive and personal journey it can become for a particular child.

Make books a safe haven, a comfort zone where kids can turn not only if they are feeling sorry for themselves, but also when they are happy, when they are tired, or when they are bored. The type of reading material recommended can also be comfortable or pain-free. Perhaps for your students, pain-free reading is reading letters or reading a diary. Perhaps it is reading comic strips. Maybe it is a book of jokes or riddles. To entice readers, it is your responsibility to make their reading relevant and fun. Comfy pillows and an area to kick off their shoes in the library or classroom will strengthen the connection between children, books, and relaxation.

Making Reading Relaxing: Sample Scenarios

Learn to counter each negative comment about reading with a positive one. Not only will this encourage the child to read, it will also make you a safe person for the reluctant reader with whom to talk.

Student: "This book is too hard for me."
Librarian: "It is an opportunity to learn words you don't know. How can I help make it easier for you?"

Student: "I don't feel like reading."
Librarian: "Maybe you'd rather be on the computer right now. It's a different kind of reading."

Student: "This book is too long."
Librarian: "Just read a page or a chapter and tell me what you think. Perhaps you'd like to read it out loud."

Student: "I'm not any good at reading."
Librarian: "Have you read any comic strips lately? Did you enjoy them? That's reading, too." (Then recommend a graphic novel.)

Focus on the 10 Cs to Fuel Students' Shelf-Esteem

There are 10 words beginning with the letter "C" that will help your students with building their Shelf-Esteem: competence, confidence, choice, communication, collaboration, coping, comfort, companions, caring, and connections.

1. Competence
One crucial method of increasing good feelings about reading is to set small, achievable goals. As you proceed step-by-step, it is important to give positive feedback at each juncture. The students need to picture themselves succeeding in order to feel **competent**, and they need to feel competent in order to actually become competent **and** make progress toward personal goals.

2. Challenge
Be sure that you continue to **challenge** students. They need to try something new because new experiences are learning experiences that can build self-confidence. Just be sure that the challenges will not defeat the student. New goals should be created in small, attainable increments.

3. Choice
As students assert themselves and make positive **choices**, they will increase their sense of themselves as readers. They will learn more, and they will increase their Shelf-Esteem, as they **choose books** from the shelves in the library. Focus on what the students *can* do, not on what they cannot do.

4. Collaboration, 5. Communication
Help students **collaborate** in discussions or activities so that they can **communicate** their interpretations or their reactions to books. The work of students is both to read and process, but they do not need to do this in isolation.

6. Coping, 7. Comfort, 8. Companions
Children are hard at work learning to solve problems and handle their emotions. That is when the model of using books to help children **cope** comes into play. Not only do books help students feel better about themselves when they read about someone who has a problem similar to theirs, they also learn the concept that every lifelong learner knows—that books are essential sources of **comfort** and good **companions** as well as sources of knowledge.

9. Caring
Caring about the characters makes readers read on to the conclusion of the book and also makes them learn to care about themselves and others.

10. Connections
Students will make **connections** between what they read and what is going on in their lives, and they will learn to transfer caring about the protagonist of a story to caring about someone they know. They will also **connect** the confident feelings from successful reading experiences to other areas of their lives and feel successful in many other endeavors.

Expect Students to Be Successful
The great chef Julia Child said she learned many things in Paris, France, but the most important was how to shop like a Parisian: "It was life-changing because shopping in France taught me about human relations." She learned that the French are highly attuned to social nuance. If a tourist enters a food store thinking she will be cheated, the salesman will happily oblige. But if he senses that his customer took a genuine interest in his produce then he would just "open up like a flower" (Prud'homme, 2004).

The lesson that Julia Child learned in Paris also applies to student-librarian (or student-teacher) relationships. If the librarian thinks of the student as a "poor reader," then the student will carry this negative label and will internalize the negativity. But, if the librarian takes a genuine interest in the student and is concerned with the student's interests and life experience, the positive personal attention the librarian exhibits will help nurture the reader in that child. An enthusiastic, curious reader will "open up like a flower."

Break Tasks into Smaller Increments

Small steps lead to great accomplishments. Be patient with your students, and offer support and encouragement each step of the way. Help them see how reading a few pages on a regular basis really adds up. Keep track of the total number of pages that the group or team reads as a whole.

Some schools have a party on the 100th day of school; reward your group with a party when they have read 100 or 1,000 pages. There is nothing wrong with a bit of healthy competition among classes or among different libraries, and among grade levels to spur readers on toward the finish line—that is, the finish line of a great book.

SPELLING SUCCESS

How Do You Foster Shelf-Esteem?

S — Show sincere interest in children's reading choices.
H — Help children honor their individuality.
E — Encourage children and exhibit their work in school and at home.
L — Let children learn from one another.
F — Foster positive attitudes.

E — Energize and emphasize engagement in reading.
S — Strengthen the bonds among home, school, and community.
T — Teach your children to work as a team, to cooperate and help each other.
E — Enjoy and encourage each child's unique talents.
E — Entertain while educating.
M — Motivate by bringing personal meaning to the text.

All aspects of Shelf-Esteem are positive. Shelf-Esteem includes self-esteem, confidence, motivation, and love of reading. It is the product of having fun, enjoying what you are doing, respecting one another, motivating children, cooperating with each other, being comfortable with the surroundings and oneself, trying new things, and enjoying and finding meaning in reading. Children who develop Shelf-Esteem are able to use books for entertainment, self-knowledge, coping strategies, comfort, information, and the discovery of more wonderful books.

References
Branden, Nathaniel. 1994. *The Six Pillars of Self-Esteem*. New York: Bantam.
Golinkoff, Roberta Michnick, Kathy Hirsh-Pasek and Diane Eyer. 2004. *Einstein Never Used Flashcards*. Emmaus, PA: Rodale.
Prud'homme, Alex. 2004. *New York Times*, August 20, 2004, page A23.

CHAPTER 17

Launching a Program

AIMING FOR SUCCESS

Now that you understand the benefits of Shelf-Esteem and the cycle that reinforces the program, it is time to concentrate on how you can transform your library or classroom into a model of Shelf-Esteem success.

Part I of this book gave you many ideas on how to build Shelf-Esteem using specific books, arranged by topic. This chapter explains principles of booktalks, activities, and discussions that are conducive to Shelf-Esteem environments and then gives examples of specific Shelf-Esteem points such as choosing materials, recognizing readers, and involving parents.

Although everything that you do and say feeds into the child's Shelf-Esteem, there are three important elements that are particularly crucial in a Shelf-Esteem program: the booktalk, the discussion, and the activity. These three elements pique—or maintain—the child's interest, help develop the motivation to read, lead to feelings of competence, and help students to connect with texts and make books an important part of their lives.

PREPARING BOOKTALKS[1]

The point of the booktalk is to interest children in a particular book, or, if you cover several books in a booktalk, to help children choose which books they would like to read. You should give just enough information about a book to make it sound enticing. "Just enough" is the key here. You never want to give away endings or tell so much about the book that the child thinks there is now no need to read it. You don't have to do all of the talking yourself. You may decide that the best way to fire up the students is to ask them what they would do in the protagonist's situation. Do whatever you think will "hook" the kids.

The two most important things to keep in mind when preparing a booktalk are (1) you want to hook your reader early, and (2) you don't want to stop until the children are dying to know what happens next. Of course, it is a given that you do not reveal the ending or any surprises.

---

[1] The author is indebted to Jennifer Bromann (*Booktalking That Works*. New York: Neal-Schuman, 2001) for information on booktalks. This book is an excellent source for practical advice on booktalks and provides samples for a wide range for books.

You can keep the children's interest high if you vary the booktalks to fit the type of books you are discussing or take the children's preferences into consideration.

Some basic types of booktalks are plot-based booktalks, dramatizations, narratives, and mood booktalks. No matter which of these—or which combination of these—you choose, the key to a successful booktalk is that you, the person motivating the children, must be familiar with the book. You will want to be animated, excited, and enthusiastic about the book. Even if you prefer one type of booktalk over another, try all types. Remember, variety is the spice of booktalks.

Create Plot-based Booktalks and Summaries

Some books lend themselves to a brief plot summary (Norton and Anfin, 2003). When you summarize, tell just enough to pique interest in the story. Wherever possible, show how the story relates to your readers. The more the students can identify with the characters, the more they will be motivated to read the book. One way to plan a booktalk that sparks interest is to pretend that the booktalk you are writing is the end of a chapter, and it must make the reader want to turn the page to find out what happens next.

Anecdotal Technique

Another approach to plot-based booktalks is called the anecdotal technique. Here, you choose interesting details about a single incident from a story or about an entire story from an anthology (Norton and Anfin, 2003). Norton and Anfin suggest this as a good format to use with booktalks on short stories, folk tales, fables, and poetry. This is an exception to the rule about not giving away endings. Here you may give away the conclusion to one of the stories to pique students' interest in the collection as a whole, with the assumption that the students will want to read similar stories in the collection.

Craft Dramatization Booktalks (Narrative)

The dramatization booktalk focuses on a particular character in the book. The librarian or teacher actually speaks as the character would (a narrative) and engages the students with a dramatic monologue. This is limited only by your imagination. Stick figures; puppetry; use of props, such as hats, costumes; dialogue using different voices; sound effects; music; or body movements, such as stamping feet or clapping hands. Use anything you think will get the children excited about the book.

Compose Mood Booktalks

The mood type of booktalk "evokes the general atmosphere of the work" (Norton and Anfin, 2003: 209). You can do this by talking about the writer's style, certain images that the author uses, or moods that the author evokes. This is a good complement to a plot-based booktalk.

Build Self-Esteem with Booktalks

Norton and Alfin stress the importance of recognizing and honoring each child's birthday with booktalks, thereby nurturing "feelings of Self-Esteem. When combined with birthday celebrations, booktalks on literature selections related to birthdays are recommended to promote emergent literacy as well as Self-Esteem" (Norton and Anfin, 2003: 204). Also, you can honor each child's birthday by donating a book to the school or public library, with an appropriate bookplate. This builds the child's self-esteem while building the collection of the library.

DISCUSSING INTRIGUING IDEAS

Discussions are an important aspect of developing shelf-esteem. Students of all ages learn to talk in a group, taking turns and listening to others. More directly related to reading are the processes of remembering enough about the book to discuss it, relating to the characters or the situation in a way that is meaningful and feels worth sharing with others, choosing what to say and how to express it, comparing one's ideas to the ideas of others, using new words from the book in a discussion, and listening to and appropriating the vocabulary that others use to express their ideas.

Discussing books is a cyclical and self-reinforcing experience. Students have a chance to:

- remember aspects of the book they had forgotten
- realize that there are situations that they now can relate to
- feel comforted to learn that their reactions were similar to those of others in the class
- learn that they can rely on themselves to relate effectively to the content
- decide to read a book that they have not read before
- hear someone use a new word that they want to use in speech or writing

As with every aspect of helping students have positive reading experiences, discussions should be fun. You will want to make the students should feel good about their contributions. Good experiences in a class discussion will help students hone their ideas and will encourage shyer students to risk speaking aloud.

When you have a class discussion, your role is to lead or facilitate the discussion without dominating it. Ask pointed questions, particularly open-ended ones, which have no right or wrong answer. The idea is for the kids to open up and express their feelings in a safe environment. They are not being judged or graded. Always end on a hopeful note with ideas for coping strategies and positive reinforcement for positive efforts.

Discussion can also be a part of booktalks and activities. Do not discourage students from asking questions or making pertinent comments. This will only undermine your efforts to develop their Shelf-Esteem.

Formulate Questions that Encourage Discussion

When students read newspaper articles, they are told to focus on the 5Ws and the H: Who, What, Where, When, Why, and How. When reading a book for a Shelf-Esteem exercise, the students will be thinking in terms of the KCAASE (pronounce it case, as in making a case for Shelf-Esteem). KCAASE stands for Knowledge, Comprehension, Application, Analysis, Synthesis, and Evaluation. Benjamin Bloom outlines these increasingly higher-level thinking skills (Bloom, 1956), which provide an excellent outline for a discussion. You can write questions to foster these thinking skills à la Bloom, adapting the questions to the grade level and the abilities of the students.

1. Establish the level of **knowledge** of the book: What does the child know about the book, the characters, and the problems? Discuss the content so that it is fresh in the students' minds so they can answer subsequent questions.
2. Enhance **comprehension** of the book: What does the child understand about the book's purpose, its premise? Focus on **comprehension** of the text, understanding the characters'

motivations, understanding the problem and the possible solutions, and understanding the outcome of the character's actions or inactions.

3. Facilitate **application** of the book's purpose. What can the child use from his or her background knowledge to bring meaning to the book? Ask leading questions to apply the students' real-life background experiences to what they have read. What has been their experience in possibly similar situations? What have they read that would have led them to react or handle situations differently? Let the children describe or explain the events in their own words.

4. Lead the students in an **analysis** of the work: What does the child know about the structure of the book? Break down the text into its various components. What happened first, what happened next, what happened at the end of the book? How did it all happen; how does it come together?

5. Encourage **synthesis** of the book's content: What can the child learn from the book to use in his or her own situation? Promote *synthesis* of the information by having the students compare what happened in the book to real-life situations as well as to think and talk about new ideas based on the book.

6. Tie everything together with an **evaluation** of the book: What does the child think of the book, the solutions offered, and the outcome? Encourage discussion of students' opinions, inferences, and empathy with characters. Try to evoke justification for answers.

Remember that these are simply suggested guidelines. You will have ideas of your own, and the children are likely to see things in ways that are new to you. Don't squelch their ideas and their enthusiasm. It is important that they come away from the discussion with their Shelf-Esteem enhanced. If they are confident that their contributions have been heard and taken seriously, they will have the confidence to contribute to the higher-level discussions.

EXPERIMENTING WITH ACTIVITIES

Activities take students beyond the cerebral and emotional experiences of reading and enable them to experience what they have read with all of their senses. Everything from field trips to finger painting to hearing a related recording or seeing a play will contribute to a book's imprinting itself on the child's brain. Well-chosen activities will help children understand the book better because they have had the opportunity to experience what the characters experience. And, of course, when books are paired with activities that are fun, reading moves into the fun category. Writing activities will reinforce reading experiences and help foster comprehension and reading fluency.

There are no limits to the book-based activities that children will enjoy, and once you are comfortable working with Shelf-Esteem programs you will find yourself thinking up new activities-these activities will give your own creativity a boost as well. Here are some tips to get you started.

- Hook onto the concrete activities described in the book. Anything that brings the book to life is a potential activity.
- Start by focusing on the five senses. Is there a description of something to eat? What about sounds or smells that you can re-create?

- Latch on to any potential art projects that will make the book more meaningful, that will help the child develop a personal relationship with the book. Be sure to suggest art projects that are appropriate for the children's ages and skills. You want them to be successful and to feel proud of the final product.
- Role playing the various characters' parts is always a helpful dramatic technique to increase empathy. When children act out parts of a story they have the opportunity to understand the book better, to grow closer to the characters and situations in the book, and to use books as a springboard to their own imaginative play.

Examine Sample Activities

Cell Phones: The Great Communicators

Reaching students where their interests are strongest guarantees the biggest returns as far as interest and effort are concerned. Cell phones are today's favorite appendage of youth. We would like books to be in the other back pocket, in that enviable spot of carry-ability. Assign characters in books vanity cell phone numbers and have conversations among the characters of the books your class has chosen to read, using cell phones as props. You can start out with dialogue from the text and then expand these conversations so that the students supply original words for the characters.

Text messaging is another technique that can be used to encourage students to get inside the character's minds. How can the feelings of the characters be transmitted via a text message?

E-mails to the Characters

Children love nothing better than to send and receive e-mail messages and instant messages on the computer. Have children work in teams, where the members of each team will choose to read the same book, chapter by chapter. One child on each team will take the part of an interviewer, and the other will be one of the characters. The child who is the interviewer will ask the character questions, and the child who is the character will answer in the guise of that character. They will conduct all of the interviews by e-mail. When the interviews have been completed, print out the e-mails for the class to read and discuss. As a treat, IM (instant messaging) sessions may also be held for fun, perhaps once a week.

Send an E-mail Full of Confidence

Computer technology makes it easier to communicate encouraging messages to your students. On the www.crayola.com Web site, there are cards of encouragement and support in various categories that you can send. There even are cards to send to "Book Lovers" with messages such as "Reading a good book and thinking of you," or cards to "Encourage a beginning writer." Send messages out to your students today. They will not only appreciate the message, they will associate reading with getting positive attention from you.

SELECTING MATERIALS TO ENHANCE A SHELF-ESTEEM PROGRAM

Librarians and teachers are in the enviable position of being able to assist young readers in their search for the appropriate reading material. You have broad influence and a formidable wide-ranging path to choose. You also have a responsibility to try to find the right book for the right child at the right time. In addition to the tips on how to select certain genres, you will also want to consider the following criteria:

- past experiences with a particular genre or author
- interest levels
- relevance of a topic to the child's current mood and emotional state
- peer influence
- parental influence

Remember, you are not selecting books for an "average" ten-year-old. You are selecting books for a particular child at a particular point in his or her development. The child's feelings about being a capable reader, being a capable person, and subsequent performance in school can be greatly influenced by book choices.

Know Your Kids

Knowing your kids will guide you in your book selection because you will help your students gravitate toward those books they *want* to read. Having a selection of books to choose from gives the child a sense of control over his or her choice. This means providing an abundance of books in a variety of genres. Likewise, the more Shelf-Esteem booktalks, discussions, and activities you can provide, the more comfortable the students will be in selecting their own reading material.

It cannot be stated too often that you need to know your students to create goals that they can attain and that they will want to reach. One way of knowing your kids is to gather interest-inventory-information, enlisting the help of the parents in that regard. Distribute publishers' catalogs and promotional materials and ask children to circle any books that interest them. This will not only help you with ordering information for collection development, but it will give you valuable information about your group's interests. Then have children cut up the catalogs and make a collage of books they'd like to read. Send questionnaires about student's reading interests at home to parents and make determining their personal life stages and interests a collaborative effort.

Communication between home and school is very helpful in getting to know children's interests. Sending Shelf-Esteem journals back and forth between home and school will clue teachers and parents in to events in students' lives that would be augmented by various readings. Habits can be created so that parents automatically write about upcoming crucial events, trips, or family matters. Then, teachers can be on the right track with offerings of relevant books that will tie in with students' interests and concerns. If a child is having difficulty at the playground in the afternoon with a bully, the parent can inform the teacher of this situation, and then the librarian/teacher can be on the lookout for a book, such as *King of the Playground* by Phyllis Naylor that deals with that issue. Similarly, if the teacher notices that the child is having a problem with a bully at the school playground, the book might be suggested or even sent home with the child for further reinforcement.

Interest inventories (questionnaires) can be sent out at the beginning of the school year to get a basic picture of the student's outside interests and activities. This form will ask about students' interests outside of school, extracurricular activities, family composition, reading habits, magazine subscriptions the child receives, how often the family visits the library. Then when a child is in the school library and is having difficulty finding a book, the librarian will be better equipped to guide the child in the right direction. This interest inventory should be updated a few times during the year, to reflect changes at home. Teachers and librarians should be on the lookout for possible "hooks" to student interests, such as talents the child exhibits, instruments played, sports involvement after school, lessons taken such as dance, and family cultural traditions that might interest the child.

Having the children write autobiographies or dictate information will also give educators additional insight into the lives of the students outside of school and will help with book selection, home collaboration, and will foster parental involvement in book choices.

Choose the Appropriate Reading Mood

Encourage children to choose the type of reading they wish to do according to their mood and the time of day. For example, the book they want to read at bedtime will not necessarily be the book they want to read at school. Remind children to choose from the wide variety of books available, similar to the choices they make when they listen to music or watch television. Biographies, poetry, mysteries, folklore, fairy tales, humorous books, comics or graphic novels, fiction, nonfiction, picture books are all genres to explore and are part of a balanced reading diet. The more types of books children are exposed to and the more reading material they become interested in, the more motivated they will be as they get older to read and keep on reading.

Books Preschoolers Should Be Exposed to:

1. **Storybooks**—These are traditional books that tell a story with a beginning, middle, and end.
2. **Wordless picture books**—These are valuable for their inherent storytelling and open-endedness. Helpful in making the connection between the spoken word and the written word. Have the child dictate text to accompany the illustrations, in his or her own words.
3. **Poetry books**—Start with Mother Goose and continue on to many other rhyming books.
4. **Concept books**—Use these for learning phonics and increasing phonemic awareness. These include alphabet books, books of shapes, numbers, opposites. Tana Hoban's books are good examples of concept books.
5. **Sensory books**—These books have something that is touchable, such as *Pat the Bunny* by Dorothy Kunhardt, or make sounds when the child presses the right button.
6. **Beginning readers**—These books have a limited vocabulary; the stories are often told in rhyme and include lots of white space and many illustrations.
7. **Nonfiction books**—An adult should read these aloud and explain them to the child. These are most useful for the illustrations and photographs.
8. **Collections of books by the same author**—Create a library of the child's favorite author's works, for example, Ezra Jack Keats or Eric Carle.
9. **Books written and illustrated by the child**—Using illustrations or photographs to create unique books with the child's writings (which may be dictated).
10. **Special books**—jokebooks, cookbooks, travel books. Tie these books in to relevant events in the child's life.

Make certain that adults in the child's life keep reading to them on a daily basis. Remind the parents of this every chance you get. Even after children learn how to read, the special connection between the parent or teacher, the child, and the printed word is vital. When adults read to children, they can choose more difficult material, because children will understand more difficult vocabulary when it is in context. They can learn new words when adults are there to explain it to them. Remember that children's listening vocabulary is more advanced than their speaking vocabularies.

For your younger students, check your library's copy of *A to Zoo: Subject Access to Children's Picture Books*, 6th edition, by Carolyn W. Lima. This is a very comprehensive subject guide that even includes subject headings such as Emotions—Fear, and lists of character traits: for example, Patience.

Introduce the Idea of Book Hopping

Essentially, book hopping is using a child's interest to connect one book with the next, to branch out and find different types of books at the individual child's reading level to build confidence, and to refer them to books that speak to the child's interests to provide motivation. If the child does not seem interested in a given book, look for something else that might work, something that will provide a fun experience.

Suppose you conduct an interest inventory and determine that one of the children is fascinated with spiders. You might guide the child to E. B. White's *Charlotte's Web* for a fiction choice, but after that, a nonfiction book about spiders would be a good way to continue your book-hopping. Then check the children's magazine *Spider* for an article or a poem about spiders. (*Spider*'s mascot happens to be a spider.) Next, weave a wider Web by including Spider-man in graphic-novel format or on the Internet. The possibilities are endless as long as you begin with a deep interest in your student and introduce material that is on his or her level and personally relevant.

LEADING CHILDREN TO BOOKS

As the old adage goes, "You can lead a horse to water, but you can't necessarily make him drink." Likewise, you can lead children to books, but you can't necessarily make them read. But you can pique their interest and charge their imaginations through booktalks, you can create appeal to their senses (through activities), and you can create settings (discussions) in which peer input, collaboration, and positive reinforcement will make it more likely that a desire to read will be born.

This chapter, when used with Part I, gives you the basics for creating your own Shelf-Esteem program. Enjoy it and make it your own! Above all, have fun instituting a Shelf-Esteem program that works for your library.

References

Bloom, Benjamin. 1956. *Bloom's Taxonomy of Educational Objectives*. New York: Longman.

Lima, Carolyn W. 2006. *A to Zoo: Subject Access to Children's Picture Books*, 7th edition. Westport, CT: Libraries Unlimited.

Norton, Terry L., and Carol Anfin. 2003. "Birthday Booktalks: Fostering Emergent Literacy and Self-Esteem in Young Children." *Reading Horizons* 43, no. 3, pp. 203–212.

CHAPTER 18

Using Special Topics and Projects

ARRANGE YOUR ROOM FOR SUCCESS

The physical environment of your classroom or library can either put children off or motivate them. Books need to be accessible, with many titles or covers facing out to pique interest. A cozy chair, a couch, or pillows invite reading at a moment's notice. Motivational posters displayed throughout the room are helpful, too. Interesting book jackets should be displayed, especially when new books arrive. Book reviews by professionals and by youngsters should be posted, with the displays changed periodically. Photographs of authors should be visible to remind children about the humanity of the profession, and that they can aspire to be authors, too. Make sure books are evident in every part of the room to correlate with curriculum. Books about mathematics can be located near the calculators. Books about artists can be plentiful in the corner holding art supplies. Music books, biographies of musicians, and sheet music should be overflowing in the area where instruments are kept. Books about varieties of plants should be near actual plants in the classroom. The science lab and the home economics labs should be stocked with titles about healthy eating and exercise.

Of course, displaying the children's own work is a must! And finally, the teacher's or librarian's desk should be approachable and not set apart in a way that intimidates readers.

"Table" of Contents

Have a table in your library that will offer students a choice of index cards. On each card will be the "contents" (or theme) of various books read by others in the class. By trading cards the way they trade baseball cards, students can compare what they have read and get ideas for new reading materials by consulting the table.

Display a Shelf of Esteem

Kids today desperately need heroes. What better way to introduce them to real heroes of the day than to have a shelf of books with the covers facing outward so kids can browse this shelf of esteem. Change display often and make sure you are gender- and race-sensitive.

Designate a CharicaChair (Character Chair)

Select a special chair to be the class charicachair. When you sit in this chair you become the character of the book under discussion. You talk like the character, act like him (or her), and give the group a chance to hear the character speak to them—either a monologue from the book or your own topic. Be sure to let the children take turns sitting in the charicachair to address the children as they present a character to their teammates or friends.

INVOLVING THE SENSES

The senses are a powerful means of making brain connections between what kids read and what they remember. Use these sensory activities in your classroom or library to evoke settings, plot, and characters so that books have a greater impact.

Use Different Smells

Prepare foods that are mentioned in the story. For example, cut open a lemon or an orange or make microwave popcorn. Cologne or even air freshener can trigger memories and evoke an emotional response. Individual car air fresheners work well, too.

Employ Various Sounds

Use the sense of hearing to create moods; for example, music playing in the background, sound effects, instruments, and songs can all connect readers to characters and text. Ask the readers to determine what kind of music a particular character would enjoy—or not enjoy.

Bring in Different Textures

The sense of touch—fabric, carpet, velvet, or even a smooth rock—can evoke feelings, emotions, and connections to the text. Ask the kids which things they touch remind them of the book.

Include the Sense of Taste

Take a leap of faith and try something new! Ask the kids to describe the sensation of a particular taste; have them write about it. Then ask them what the character you are examining would say about that taste. Bring in snacks mentioned in the book or snacks that a character in a book might like to eat. Create an appropriate recipe.

Draw on the Sense of Sight

Lead the class in a discussion of how the author describes the setting in terms of what it looks like. Talk also about the visual description of the characters. Now ask the kids to use the same type of visual descriptions and visual metaphors to discuss either the classroom or their environments at home.

Utilize All Five Senses to Experience Reading

Ask the kids to take a character or a setting from a favorite book and describe him or her in terms of all five senses. Have them answer questions that will pull in all of the senses. What does the character or setting look like? What tastes do they remind you of? What music would you be playing in the background as you read this book? What are the smells described in the book? What smells do you think of when you read certain passages of the book? What are the different textures mentioned in the book? Do you think of hot or cold when you read the book? Are there things you touch that remind you of the book?

> There is a boutique in Manhattan called Assouline that sells $45 candles that are scented like libraries. Ask the class what memories a candle like this would evoke. Discuss what this candle's fragrance would be like. Each person's association will be distinct. You would hope all students have positive associations about the library and books, so emphasize those.

ENCOURAGE KIDS TO KEEP ELECTRONIC LIBRARY JOURNALS

Your readers will enjoy logging on to update their library journals. These special files—either on school computers or home computers—can be decorated with electronic clip art, fancy fonts, wingdings, and scanned images tailored to the child's reading interests. This will be the childrens' personal logs of the books they have read; their reactions, questions that arose, why they liked or disliked a book, and if they would recommend it to a friend.

This journal will serve as positive reinforcement to the children because each one will tell the child's "reading story" for that year. It will also provide a fun opportunity to be creative on the computer while it serves as a writing and interpretation exercise as well. The journal will also be helpful to parents and teachers for an immediate clue to the child's interest inventory. This log will serve an awareness-raiser about the books the child is reading and, because it is a written record, it will lift the level of importance attributed to the child's reading interests. Books included can be taken out of the classroom library, the school library, and the public library as well as books that the children own.

If the kids are willing, these can be made into interactive journals into which parents and teachers can record positive comments such as, "I remember reading this book when I was your age. It was one of my favorites because I could identify with the characters." The log should become a source of pride to the child and a source of accomplishment to the child's family. Encourage the parents to maintain a special shelf at home for reading logs from previous years. They can refer to them the way they refer to photo albums to reflect on the growth of the students and to recall favorite books, grade by grade.

If there are not sufficient computer resources either at home or school for the entire class to keep online journals, have them create their own paper journals. Encourage them to decorate these journals with crayons, paints, pictures from magazines, or photos. They will be far more appealing than turning in book reports every week.

PLAY THE "GIVING TREE" LIBRARY GAME

Every time a teacher or librarian recommends a book to a child, she (or he) is offering a truly great present. You might look upon your recommendations as gifts like those given by the tree in *The Giving Tree* by Shel Silverstein (Harper & Row, 1964). When you choose a book, you are considering the childrens' interests, but you are also anticipating and enlarging upon them. The satisfaction you feel when you match the book to the child is the same satisfaction a gift giver feels upon selecting the perfect present.

Give your groups the opportunity to present books to each other with the same thoughtfulness. Pairs or teams can search for library books for each other and gift wrap them. Before they actually select the books, they should conduct interviews to discover each other's interests. This reinforces the idea that a book is a present that others can give to us or that we can give to ourselves.

TREAT LIBRARY CARDS LIKE PASSPORTS

Tell the youngsters that their library cards are truly passports to knowledge, adventure, and a broader world view. Make certain that your group has 100 percent enrollment at the public library, and that each child has his or her own public library card. Then have the children start their travels.

1. Place each child's library card in a specially created Shelf-Esteem holder, either wallet-sized or sized to hang around the neck.
2. Stamp the passport book each time a new genre is visited.
3. Include pages for fiction, nonfiction, mysteries, biographies, travel guides, folk tales, reference, poetry, plays, chapter books, or how-to manuals, according to grade level.
4. Hold an international foods party when you finish the curriculum unit, using the stamped passport as entry payment.

Be sure to make a big fuss and a public announcement over the PA system or loudspeaker when each class reaches 100 percent enrollment, just as many schools do as classes reach 100 percent enrollment in the Parent-Teacher Organization.

VISIT A VIRTUAL MUSEUM

Even if you can't physically visit a museum, you can take a "virtual trip" to many museums. For instance, the Garbage Museum in Stratford, Connecticut boasts a "trash-o-saurus," a one-ton dinosaur made out of garbage and a "sky box" view of the process of dumping and sorting—a recycling primer in action. On their Web site at www.crrra.org/, the children can read the description and then imagine what the rest of the museum must look like. Ask them what they envision the museum to look like, what features they would introduce there, why they think recycling is important, and if it makes sense to have a garbage museum. Depending on their ages, you might suggest drawing a picture of an exhibit or writing a brochure for their own Garbage Museums. Perhaps they will want to have a look at Violaine Lamerand's book *Crafts From Junk* (Bridgestone Books, 2003) to make their own recycled projects. You can lead into a discussion of how students participate in recycling at home. What types of recycling are available in your community? Is there a local trash to energy plant you might be able to visit?

In this case, the name Garbage Museum is the hook to pique their interest. Once they have become motivated to learn more about the museum and its mission, you have paved the way for your children to want to learn more on their own. Getting into the habit of finding out more, of doing researching just because you want to find something out, and of taking book knowledge and applying it to real life is the true message of Shelf-Esteem. The more children learn, the more they will want to learn.

SET UP YOUR OWN MUSEUM EXHIBITS

You can also decide to set up an exhibit of your own in the library. The children can prepare their own items to place in the exhibit. For example, you could take an idea from the Spertus Museum in Chicago, which in 2005 hosted an exhibit called Every Picture Tells a Story. The exhibit was created and organized by the Breman Museum in Atlanta, Georgia (www.the breman.org/), and the Every Picture Tells a Story gallery in Santa Monica, California (www.everypicture.com/). The exhibit used illustrations from classic and contemporary children's books to impart messages to children about diversity, tolerance, ethical behaviors, and self-esteem.

You can help your readers create an exhibit (in your library or classroom) of illustrations that they feel represent these same important messages. The children might also want to look at the Every Picture Tells a Story Web site to discuss the pictures found there to use as models.

CHAPTER 19
====================

Finding Shelf-Esteem Partners

PUT THE SHOW ON THE ROAD

While teachers and librarians have the most important tools for building Shelf-Esteem—books and contact with the children—the activities that contribute to this growth are not confined to the school. In addition to the crucial role that parents play, there are a wealth of resources available in your community and on the Web. As Jane Beirn, a director of publicity at HarperCollins says, "Any kind of fresh way to attract people to books is exciting" (Rich, 2006: E1).

Students also need to collaborate with each other. Teamwork allows students to help each other, a win-win situation for the helper as well as the one helped. Collaboration between students is as important as collaboration between institutions. In her book *The School Buddy System: The Practice of Collaboration*, Gail Bush elaborates on collaboration and how to achieve it (Bush, 2002).

COLLABORATING WITH MUSEUMS

Museums are always fun outings, but they can also be your partners in helping children develop Shelf-Esteem. Combining a trip to a local or virtual museum with books, activities, and discussion is an excellent way to help children become more confident learners. Remember:

Interest + Motivation = Learning

You can do a museum talk—like a booktalk but with an exhibit as the hook—so the children will start to think about what they are going to see. They might want to draw some pictures of something on display, and, then, once they are back at the library or back at school, find some books that either explain more about what they have seen or use what they have seen as a backdrop for reading fiction or nonfiction. Be sure to check with the museum's educational or outreach office to see if their docents have special programs for children. For example, Dr. Kathy Hirsh-Pasek, co-author of *Einstein Never Used Flashcards*, has acted as an adviser to the Children's Museum of Manhattan in their National Family Play and Learning

Initiative, PlayWorks. "PlayWorks is designed to foster not only literacy, but also mathematical understanding and cultural literacy." Leslie Bushara, deputy director for education of the Children's Museum in Manhattan said, "We wanted a place where looking at words and letters was fun and could build the foundation for sitting together and reading books" (Graeber, 2006: E3). Joann Norrisk's *Children's Museums: An American Guidebook* (McFarland, Jefferson, NC, 1998) gives information on museums by state.

COLLABORATING AND COMMUNICATING AMONG SCHOOLS

Not only can you expose your students to far more if you work with other schools, but you will also be reassuring them that they are learning to cope with groups beyond their own schools, homes, and families. Communication among schools on all levels, is a pre-requisite to a unified Shelf-Esteem program. You will want the youngsters to move on to middle school and high school without losing their enthusiasm for reading and learning and their confidence in their ability to do it.

So, for example, if there is going to be a book fair or literacy night at the middle school in your district, make sure that the elementary and high schools are invited as well. Keep a master calendar so that schools are not competing with one another. You don't want an author night at one venue to coincide with a book fair at another. Not only will you lose part of your audience, it will be frustrating for students to have to choose between equivalent options.

Do not leave the preschools in your area out of the mix. Make sure they receive flyers about books sales, authors' nights, and read-aloud times in the library. As soon-to-be kindergarteners, they need to be exposed to these literacy activities.

Another reason for communication among schools is that the library reaches the widest range of reading levels for a given age group. One fifth-grader may need to attend a book fair at the high school to find books on her reading and interest level, but another sixth-grader may very well need elementary school books. Cross-pollination also helps kids to feel more comfortable attending the school on the next level up and to familiarize them with the school library and the librarian. What is familiar becomes what is comfortable, and what is comfortable makes students feel empowered and secure.

COLLABORATING BETWEEN HOME AND SCHOOL

One of the most important types of collaboration is the one between home and school. In addition to encouraging parents to read to their children and discuss books with them, there are also more formal types of collaboration that work. For example, a local school district might be offering a series of workshops for parents on how children learn, how parents are the first teachers, and how children build knowledge of the world.

To make such workshops more effective, the school district might offer free dinner and awards to parents who attend all three programs and free babysitting services to boot. Children are not the only ones who respond positively to incentives, such as awards. Furthermore, offering to remove barriers (such as providing free meals and free childcare) eliminate busy parents' excuses for not attending these valuable programs.

Initiate Parent-Teacher Conferences

You can use the parent-teacher conference to learn more about the child's current interests and to instruct parents in ways that they can continue to foster Shelf-Esteem in their children at home. School librarians can play an important part in the evaluation process of every reader and may be consulted prior to conferences for valuable information. Each time a parent comes to the library or to school for a conference, discuss the child's changing interests at home. What is the child currently reading? What books have they recently purchased or taken out of the school or public library? Send home a Shelf-Esteem Interest form before the conference asking these questions so that parents can come into the library or the school prepared to discuss them with you. If they don't know what their child is reading, this will remind them to ask the child. Suggest that parents occasionally read the same books, articles, or magazines as the child so that they have common ground for discussion.

Start Parent-Child Book Clubs

Just as book clubs foster discussion and a connection among their members, exclusive parent-child book clubs builds connections between parents and children. First, parents display interest in what their child is reading. Next, the parent models reading behavior by reading some of the same books that their child is reading. This offers a window of opportunity to discuss the books and the characters and what they mean to the child. Present this idea to parents during conferences, parents' night or Young Authors night at your school or library.

COLLABORATING WITH BOOK VENDORS AND BOOK FAIR EVENTS

One way to encourage children to keep reading is to reward them with books of their own. You might reward reading with tokens that children can "spend" at a school or library's annual book fair or book sale. Is it possible to fill up a giant "vending" machine with books so children can use their tokens to buy books? Look for corporate sponsors to sponsor such an event.

Another way to do this is to hold a "silent auction" for books, using tokens as payment. If you are unable to acquire new books, you can always seek donations from students, parents, teachers, and community members. Public libraries are always weeding their collections, and you can obtain books at a very nominal cost—sometimes even for free.

Of course, you can always arrange for publishers or vendors to set up a book fair with books that children can purchase for reasonable prices. The idea is to reward the positive associations that students have with books with more books so they will stay on a direct path to reading and developing more Shelf-Esteem.

COLLABORATING WITH PUBLIC TELEVISION

Reading Rainbow is a program that has been connecting children and books since 1983. "Children who watch the program feel better about themselves as people and as readers," says Yessenia Garcia-Lebron, former coordinator of WHYY's Children's Service in Philadelphia. "Children also gain confidence as readers by writing their own stories."

In partnership with the Free Library of Philadelphia, WHYY has sponsored the Reading Rainbow Young Writers and Illustrators Contest for students in grades K, 1, 2, and 3, a national competition. According to the published contest rules, the stories could be fact or fiction, prose or poetry, and they could also have math or science themes. They have to be accompanied by five clear, original, colorful illustrations. For children who could not yet write, someone else could transcribe the dictated story. Invented spelling is acceptable. Each national winner's story is posted on the Reading Rainbow Web Site (pbskids.org/reading rainbow). The winners received a library set of ten Reading Rainbow episodes and related feature books.

Why not adapt this type of contest and hold a similar one in your library or school? Post winning stories on the school Web site and offer books and DVDs as prizes. If the school district has a public radio or TV station, see if they will sponsor the contest, or at least provide air time for the winning entries.

CONNECTING SCHOOLS AND THE PUBLIC LIBRARY

The connection between schools and public libraries needs to be fostered because of the enormous potential it holds for students and their communities. Because both are educational institutions, there should be a strong alliance and a solid reliance on one another. Technology tie-ins are possible between the two locations, and thereby resources can be shared. Expensive reference works need not be purchased for both locations. Since such sharing will diminish duplication of effort, the taxpayers in the community will benefit financially, and the community's leaders will be more supportive. A vital part of the success of the Shelf-Esteem program is based on the promotion of a 100 percent rate of student ownership of public library cards.

In the public's eye, the collaboration will make the library more viable if the students are using the library resources more efficiently because of the partnership. Within the school, the school librarian must make a special effort to collaborate with the teachers to supplement and enrich the curriculum. Collaboration must also exist between the school and home to reinforce and enhance the priority of reading, discussing, and valuing books. Just a simple act of making sure that every single child in school has a valid library card ensures that the door is open for transactions.

FORGING LINKS WITH CHARITABLE ORGANIZATIONS

There are many organizations that offer great opportunities for teachers and librarians to volunteer their services. The Shelf-Esteem concept is as important to adults in literacy programs as it is for kids. They need to learn to enjoy reading; they have to be motivated; they need reading materials that are of interest to them. Also, this is something you can tell the class about—they will be interested in the idea of adults who *want* to learn to read, and they will learn to value community service.

The Organization for Rehabilitation Training (ORT) has "Educating for Life" as part of its logo. They are entering their 125th year, and their specific mission is about giving people self-esteem. In a newsletter on their website, they say: "ORT isn't about giving handouts: it's about giving self-esteem. Helping individuals achieve self-sufficiency through education and training can help them to earn their livelihood with dignity" (www.waort.org). The goals and philosophies of ORT on education reflect the vision of Shelf-Esteem principles in that ORT believes that if you help a man fish, he has food for a day, but if you teach a man to fish, he has food a lifetime. Similarly, if you help children regard reading in this new way, they will enjoy books for a lifetime.

Many organizations, such as A Woman's Place and Volunteers in Teaching Alternatives (VITA), strive to teach their charges to read, to learn to earn a living, and to achieve a feeling of self-esteem. Libraries can take a role in pairing with these local organizations to offer Shelf-Esteem exercises to the people who need to reconnect their lives to books and to education. Prison libraries would be a good place to start this process of rehabilitation through books. The Shelf-Esteem program might be useful in such a setting as a springboard to help illiterate persons develop an enthusiasm for reading.

Similarly, a new project has begun by the Legal Aid Society in New York. They have developed Reading Rooms for children, "colorfully furnished and lined with books the children can take home," said Louise Feld, a lawyer for the Legal Aid Society. Their goal is to make a visit to family court a little "less daunting for children who can be in horrible situations." A foster grandparent from New York's Department of Aging, Louise Rogers, said that "The children's hardships are so distressing (from domestic violence to dealing with foster care) that she is thrilled to read to the children, listen to their stories, and help them identify the right books for their age" (Simpson, 2006).

TAKING A CUE FROM THE ZOO: USE READING BYTES

Consider collaboration with zoos as well. After all, these are the places families visit together, and there are opportunities all around to reinforce reading goals. Being observant is all that is required. For every animal on exhibit, there is likely to be an informative sign. And some zoos have very creative ways of getting people to read information. For example, a recent visit to the National Zoo in Washington, D.C., uncovered a really useful way to promote reading. In the rest rooms, above each hand dryer, there was a placard with an interesting fact about a zoo animal. Without wasting a moment of your time, these informative signs encouraged reading—even while drying your hands. They also reinforced the priority of the zoo to give information to its visitors in unique ways. These were "reading bytes" instead of sound bytes, and the chance of retaining the information was great because of the unique way it was presented and because it was offered in small portions. Children who cannot read yet are likely to ask the parent what the sign says.

Why not incorporate this technique in school or library buildings? Kids are used to seeing advertising all over their world, from TV ads to billboards to newspaper ads. But how often do they see books and information about books advertised? This is another way to elevate the level of awareness of books in your school or library and to promote reading in a way that the advertising community has successfully used for years.

You might also want to see if a docent from a local zoo can bring some smaller animals to the school or library, or if there are special tours for school children. These are excellent jump-starts for the children to read, write about a favorite animal, and learn to spell the name of a favorite animal, draw pictures and perhaps label them. The next step is to find relevant books, a fertile field for book hopping. Of course, if your zoo has not yet developed an educational outreach program, you can still enlist parents to help with a field trip to the zoo and follow up with the same Shelf-Esteem lessons.

COLLABORATING WITH TEACHER EDUCATION PROGRAMS

Teacher training and development programs need to be aware of and informed about the Shelf-Esteem program so that they can promote the social and emotional development of readers. This can include opportunities to visit classes with teachers and librarians who foster Shelf-Esteem as well as sending these teachers and librarians to speak to training and continuing education programs. This type of collaboration will benefit future generations as well as the students of today.

COLLABORATING WITH SCHOOL PRINCIPALS AND ADMINISTRATORS

Building principals need to be informed about the Shelf-Esteem program so that their support, involvement, and encouragement can be felt by all members of the learning community—students, teachers, and parents alike. Refer to the document "Leading Early Childhood Learning Communities: What Principals Should Know and Be Able to Do" available on the Web site of the National Association of Elementary School Principals (www.naesp.org). The executive director, Dr. Vincent L. Ferrandino, explains that the gap between the incoming preschool population and the elementary school principals needs to be closed. "Principals can provide important information to early childhood program providers regarding what the expectations of the students are from the school's point of view—skills, attitudes, and behaviors. Preschool providers can provide information on social-emotional development and academic accomplishments. One informs the other" (Ferrandino, 2006).

SETTING NO LIMITS

Just as there are no limits on the activities or discussions that reading books can engender, there is no limit on the organizations with which you can collaborate. There are some obvious links, such as libraries or museums, but do not let yourself stop there. Look at TV, charitable organizations with educational missions, others in your school or school district. Any organization that cares about children, reading, or children's self-esteem is a likely candidate for collaboration. Also, be on the lookout for grants that you might be eligible for or local sponsors (including local merchants) for your reading programs. Broaden the shelf-esteem spirit as far as you can. The sky's the limit. Aim high and the results will be more rewarding than you ever thought possible. Begin your journey with confidence, a book in hand, and a smile on your face.

References
Bush, Gail. 2002. *The School Buddy System: The Practice of Collaboration.* Chicago: American Library Association.

Ferrandino, Vincent L. 2005a. "Leading Early Childhood Learning Communities: What Principals Should Know and Be Able to Do." National Association of Elementary School Principals: Alexandria, VA. Available at www.naesp.org.

Ferrandino, Vincent L. 2005b. "Getting Elementary School Principals Involved in Readiness," *Preschool Matters* 3, no. 3 (June/July): 9–11. Available at www. nieer.org.

Graeber, Laurel. 2006. "Does an Educational Exhibition Have to Be Dryly Serious? Fuggedaboudit." *New York Times*, August 8, p. E3.

Rich, Motoko. 2006. "Authors Meet Fans Far from Bookstore, at Company Event." *New York Times*, May 16, p. E1.

Simpson, April. 2006. "Shelter from the Storm: A Children's Reading Room at Family Court." *New York Times*, August 9, p. B3.

PART III

Shelf-Esteem Sources and Support

Resources
for Selecting Books

The American Library Association
www.ala.org
50 East Huron Street
Chicago, Illinois 60611
  • Notable Children's Books

The Child Study Children's Book Committee
www.bnkst.edu
Bank Street College
610 West 112 Street
New York, New York 10025
  • Children's Books of the Year
  • Paperback Books for Children, A Selected List
    through Age 13

The Horn Book, Inc.
www.hbook.com
56 Roland Street, Suite 200
Boston, Massachuseets 02109
  • Children's Classics: A Book List for Parents

The International Reading Association
www.reading.org
800 Barksdale Rd.
P.O. Box 8139
Newark, Delaware 19714
  • Children's Choices

The Library of Congress
www.loc.gov
Children's Literature Center
101 Independence Ave., S.E.
Washington, D.C. 20540
  • Books for Children

New York Public Library
Office of Branch Libraries
www.nypl.org
455 Fifth Avenue
New York, New York 10016

Children's Book Council
www.cbcbooks.org
12 West 37 Street
New York, New York 10018
  • Outstanding Science Trade Books for Children
  • Notable Children's Trade Books in the Field of
    Social Studies
  • Caldecott and Newbery Award Winners

School Library Journal
www.slj.com
360 Park Ave. So.
New York, New York 10010

BOOKS

Books to Help Children Cope with Separation and Loss
Masha Kabakow Rudman, Ed.
R. R. Bowker, 1993

Books Kids Will Sit Still For 3: A Read-Aloud Guide
Judy Freeman
Libraries Unlimited, 2006

Choosing Books for Children: A Commonsense Guide, 3rd Ed.
Betsy Hearne
University of Illinois Press, 1999

Choosing Books for Kids: How to Choose the Right Book for the Right Child at the Right Time
Joanne Oppenheim, Barbara Brenner, and Betty Boegehold
Ballantine, 1986

Family Storybook Reading
Denny Taylor and Dorothy Strickland
Heinemann, 1986

For Love of Reading: A Parent's Guide to Encouraging Young Readers from Infancy through Age 5
Masha Kabakow Rudman and Anna Markus Pearce, Eds.
Consumers Union, 1988

For Reading Out Loud! A Guide to Sharing Books with Children
Margaret Mary Kimmel and Elizabeth Segel
Dell, 1991

For Reading Out Loud: Planning & Practice
Bobbi Fisher and Emily Fisher Medvic
Heinemann, 2003

Games for Reading: Playful Ways to Help Your Child Read
Peggy Kaye
Pantheon, 1984

How to Choose Good Books for Kids
Kate McMullan
Addison-Wesley, 1984

The New Read-Aloud Handbook. 6th Ed.
Jim Trelease
Penguin, 2006

The New York Times Parent's Guide to the Best Books for Children, 3rd Ed.
Eden Ross Lipson
Three Rivers Press, 2000

Ready, Set, Read: Best Books to Prepare Preschoolers
Ellen Mahoney and Leah Wilcox
Scarecrow, 1985

A Teacher's Guide to Children's Books
Nancy Larrrick
Merrill, 1986

Valerie & Walter's Best Books for Children, A Lively, Opinionated Guide. 2nd Ed.
Walter M. Mayes and Valerie Lewis
Quill, 2004

Author and Illustrator Index

SOURCE C

Title Index

Subject Index

About the Author

Sandra Kitain holds a Masters Degree in Education and has completed a second Masters Degree in Library Science from Clarion University. She received her undergraduate degree and graduate degrees in Education from Queens College of the City University of New York. She has worked in public schools, in public and school libraries, and for publishing companies as a writer and editor. Her biographies of young adult authors may be seen in the recent publication, *The Continuum Encyclopedia of Young Adult Literature*. She has served as a reviewer for *School Library Journal* and for the Children's Book Council, and she continues to write and to present workshops at local schools and colleges for parents and teachers about literacy. She is a part-time scorer of teacher's exams for the Educational Testing Service, and has served as a peer reviewer for the Improving Literacy Through School Library Programs for the United States Department of Education since 2003.

Sandra resides in Bucks County, Pennsylvania, with her husband Howard and amid bookcases filled with books. She still reads to children and adults whenever the opportunity arises. Sandra was previously employed as a literacy/ESL coach at the Walt Disney Elementary School in Levittown, Pennsylvania. Sandra is a member of the PaLA, the ALA, NCTE, IRA, the Bucks County Librarians Association, the Children's Literature Association, and the Keystone State Library Association, and is a supporter of USBBY (U.S. Board on Books for Young People). A two-time recipient of the Ezra Jack Keats Award for the Bucks County Free Library, she also was awarded a scholarship from Boyds Mill Press to attend the PaLA Conference. Most recently, Sandra was the recipient of an ALA's "Picturing America" grant for a Pennsbury District elementary school. At present, she is fulfilling her interest in the arts by participating in the 2007 docent program at the James A. Michener Museum in Doylestown, Pennsylvania. Her hobbies include reading, traveling, yoga, cooking, attending the theater, going to the beach, and spending time with her family and friends.